Magnificat PROCLAIMS

I0087049

FATHER
KEVIN'S
KORNER

Newsletter Articles
by Fr. Kevin Scallon, C.M.

Magnificat CST Spiritual Advisor
2002–2017

ISBN: 978-1-941514-15-3 (Paperback edition)
ISBN: 978-1-941514-16-0 (eBook edition)

Magnificat is an obedient daughter of the Church and will defer to the judgment of the Holy See regarding private revelations, apparitions, and other such matters. Until then, the Second Vatican Council urges us to discern the Spirit in the case of such extraordinary graces [*Lumen Gentium* 12], which means being neither gullible or incredulous, but subjecting them to all relevant theological and human tests of credibility. Some of these experiences may help one have a closer walk with the Lord, providing they are not contrary to the faith and morals of the Church.

In August 2011, Fr. Kevin Scallon publicly withdrew his support for Direction for our Times (DFOT). Please note his articles on pages 28, 31, 32 and 44 were written prior to 2011.

Foreword

Father Kevin was a true treasure to all of us in Magnificat, as well as all who knew him! Before I personally met him, I "knew" him! I was praying for God to send to my dear friend and sister in Christ, Sr. Briege McKenna, C.S.C. a priest to accompany her. The Lord was sending her to minister His love to His people, especially priests. My husband, Pete, had become a brother in Christ to her. He suggested the Lord would want to give her the protection and counsel of a priest to travel with her. I had the same sense and began to pray earnestly that God would reveal that person. An image was revealed to me as I prayed!

A few weeks passed and Sr. Briege came to visit us in our home in New Orleans, as she often did. However, this time she brought two Irish priests with her. As they walked in the door, I immediately recognized one of them as the man I saw in prayer weeks before! I quietly drew Sr. Briege aside and whispered to her, "he is the one!" She smiled and showed her agreement! There began an instant rapport and friendship between us! He soon became close not only to Pete and I but our whole family!

Fr. Kevin was one of 15 children in his own family in Ireland, so he easily fit into our growing family! Our children, grandchildren and extended family just loved him. The children love him, even our son-in-laws would love to sneak out with him after a family Mass or dinner to go to a movie, always followed by a stop at an ice cream parlor! He was truly a holy priest as well as a very whole person!

Before the tragedy of our dear Fr. Harold Cohen's death, Magnificat's first holy and wonderful Spiritual Advisor, he and Fr. Kevin made a private retreat together! It was, as a Central Service Team (CST) member suggested, like the baton was being passed from one holy priest to another! We were delighted when he accepted the invitation from the CST to become our Spiritual Advisor and thrilled when he said he would be happy to write a column for our Magnificat Newsletter! What a gift he has been to us over the years! His timely articles and his great wit and spiritual advice have benefited us so much over the years! It is fitting that we bring together "Father Kevin's Korner" in a book as a tribute to him and a treasure to us all!

Marilyn Quirk
Magnificat, Founding Coordinator

Magnificat has been proclaiming the greatness of the Lord since 1981. This international apostolate started from humble beginnings in New Orleans, LA. On October 7, Feast of the Holy Rosary, the first Magnificat Meal was held.

The *Magnificat* (Luke 1:46–55) is the great hymn of praise that Mary prayed while visiting Elizabeth. Both women had been deeply touched by God. Elizabeth was bearing a long-awaited child; Mary was carrying within her womb the very Son of God. They came together to help one another, to speak of God's action in their lives, to sing, to pray, to share a common table, and to be strengthened for all that was to come.

Magnificat came into being out of a desire to share with all Catholic women the fruit we have experienced through the Catholic Charismatic Renewal. We describe this fruit as:

- a deeper knowledge and love of Jesus Christ
- an experience of the release of the power of the Holy Spirit
- an appreciation and love for Mary, our Mother and Model
- an appreciation and love for the Catholic Church

Magnificat Meals are hosted by local Chapters worldwide about every three months on or around a feast day of Mary, to whom we consecrate this ministry in a special way. We call our Meals "Magnificat" because, like Mary and Elizabeth, we want to come together in God's presence. May we too recognize what God has already done in us and call forth in each other a new openness to the power of His Spirit in our lives.

Magnificat® Central Service Team, Inc.
1629 Metairie Road—Suite 3, Metairie, LA 70005-3926
Tel: (504) 828-MARY [6279]
magnificatcst@aol.com ❖ www.magnificat-ministry.org
Facebook: MagnificatMinistry Twitter: MagnificatCST
Instagram: magnificatcst

5

This work is dedicated to
MARY
daughter of the Father,
mother of the Son,
spouse of the Holy Spirit!

Acknowledgements

We would like to thank all those who have played a part in bringing this book together. Our appreciation goes to the Magnificat Central Office staff (Cindy Delger, Jill Arteaga and Sheila Casadaban) for digging into the archives for Fr. Kevin's articles and pictures. Special thanks to the Magnificat Newsletter Team (Joan Lococo, Paulette Renaudin and Elise Botch) for bringing Fr. Kevin's words to print over the years! We would also like to extend our gratitude to Fr. Kevin's secretary, Jackie Grchan, for being so instrumental in getting his articles to press in a timely fashion.

The layout of this beautiful book from cover to cover has been made possible by our gifted graphic artist, Cathy Behrens (www.cbgraphicdesigns.com). We are most grateful to her for sharing her time and talent with Magnificat, A Ministry to Catholic Women.

It is our sincere hope that Fr. Kevin's insights will continue to bless all those who read this compilation.

Introduction

For sixteen years, Fr. Kevin Scallon, C.M. served as Spiritual Advisor and loyal friend to the Central Service Team of Magnificat, A Ministry to Catholic Women. He will long be loved and remembered by Magnificat worldwide as a gentle, loving Father with an Irish accent, great sense of humor and a twinkle in his eyes. Fr. Kevin was a faithful teacher of the Word and Catholic doctrine, well acquainted with Papal encyclicals, devoted to Blessed Mother Mary, and always ready to answer questions about living out our faith.

Fr. Kevin loved the priesthood, being a priest and ministering to brother priests. He is one of the nineteen contributing authors in our second book in the Magnificat Proclaims series called Holy Orders, A Collection of Inspiring Clergy Testimonies. To read more about the life, wit and wisdom of this very special man, treat yourself to this amazing book.

It is the great desire of the Central Service Team (CST) to pay tribute to Fr. Kevin with this simple presentation of his contributions to the Magnificat Ministry Newsletters in his regular column Father Kevin's Korner. We understand that it was a real joy for him to serve the ministry in this way. It is our joy to share Fr. Kevin with you!

Magnificat Central Service Team
Donna Ross, Sara Ford, Jackie France,
Kim Rodriguez-Torres, and Mary Wilson

April 2002

The grace of our Lord be with us forever.

I would like first of all to take this opportunity to thank Marilyn Quirk and the members of the Central Service Team for asking me to be your spiritual advisor. I feel genuinely honored to be asked to do so. I have undertaken to celebrate Mass for your intentions every Saturday and will keep you before the Lord in all my prayers.

As we celebrate Christ's victory over sin and death in this Easter Season, we are also conscious of the great crisis affecting the Church at its highest level, namely its Bishops and priests. It would be easy for me to write to you and simply ignore all of this, were it not for the critical nature of the crisis and the very great scandal that it is to the people of God. These scandals have affected all of us including the faithful priests who give themselves so generously for the service of the church. It seems to me that the first step in trying to remedy this situation is to acknowledge the great offense given to Almighty God because of the sins of priests against children and young people. This is a very grave offense to the Lord bordering on the sacrilegious. For this reason I am convinced that the first step to take in remedying the situation is to offer sincere prayer and reparation to the heavenly Father in order to beg his forgiveness and healing.

It is disappointing, to say the least, that no one has yet called on the faithful to pray for this grave situation. This clearly indicates a lack of faith. It's as though people no longer believe that prayer could help to deliver the church from such a great evil.

From the Church's teaching and tradition on vicarious suffering we know that the Lord asks all of us to make reparation for our personal sins. But frequently he asks specially chosen groups and victim souls to make reparation and atonement, "To make up what is wanting to the sufferings of Christ." They do this through prayer, penance and the acceptance of suffering for their own sins and for the sins of others who refuse to repent.

Knowing that you are people who believe in the efficacy of prayer, I would like to appeal to you to begin this work of spiritual combat. In order that the church be delivered from this evil, I urge you to pray that Jesus who "lives always to intercede for us" (Hebrews 7:25) would present our prayers and good works to the Father.

The Meaning of Reparation

We sin, when through willful thoughts, desires, actions or omissions, we violate the law of God. Sin wounds the sinner, our neighbor and the whole Church. In the Sacrament of Reconciliation our sins are forgiven, but the effect of our sinfulness remains. Through penance we show our sorrow and our willingness to make reparation to God, to implore his mercy and forgiveness upon ourselves and on the Church. People sometimes find the concept of reparation difficult to grasp. A simple example may help. Suppose you rear-end someone's new Mercedes in traffic causing a couple of thousand dollars' worth of damage. You may tell the owner you are sorry and he may accept your contrition. That, however, would not be enough. The car will have to go to the body shop where it will be made as good as new again; and you, or someone else, would have to pay for it. That is reparation.

How to Make Reparation

We can do this through prayer, penance and good works. We present ourselves humbly before God, begging his forgiveness and mercy. Reparation appeases the justice of God. It is a work of mercy which helps the living and frees souls from purgatory. It brings salvation to those who are in rebellion against God and the Church.

Ways of Making Reparation

1. For ourselves we make reparation through regular recourse to the Sacrament of Reconciliation.
2. Through prayers of reparation for ourselves and others. A good example of this prayer can be found in the Book of Daniel 9:3–19.
3. Have Masses of reparation offered for the specific intention.
4. Try to get your priest to celebrate these Masses with the

people of your parish.

5. Call on our Lady of Fatima to pray for us and for our intention.
6. Pray more earnestly, fast and care for the poor.
7. Pray for one hour before the Blessed Sacrament and involve others in doing the same.
8. Go on pilgrimage.

Prayer changes things in ways that nothing else can and the prayer of reparation and repentance can accomplish great change. As we come before God seeking his mercy and healing regarding the wounds of the young and the sinfulness of some priests, we should have great confidence in his merciful forgiveness. All of these prayers we place in the Immaculate Heart of Mary, our Mother.

Conclusion

I often recall the words of our Holy Father, Pope John Paul II some years ago when he said, "now is the time for the Pope to suffer." From then on his health went into steady decline though his mind and his spirit soared. When I look at him now it is easy for me to see Christ on the cross. I remembered this when I recently read this fascinating quotation from the book Wherever He Goes by Pere Dominique Philippe, O.P. He describes Jesus in his final week of life. He says, apart from prayer, Jesus remains silent even on the cross. He writes, "The church places herself on the cross today in order to save humanity; for the church is bound to the fate of Christ. She, therefore, accepts to live out the agony, the cross, and the sepulchre … this is a great mystery. The silent church is the church in the sepulchre. Even where the church is not properly the 'silent church' she hangs on the cross. She hangs on the cross with all the discordant voices making themselves heard, so that many of the faithful no longer know where to go: one group here saying this, others over there saying something else … And everyone asking where is the truth? There were similar discordant voices at the cross."

Perhaps this is the way it has to be and that in our country, the church is now hanging on the cross. The church is held up before our eyes, upon the cross. What then is the crucified Christ saying to us Catholics today? I believe he is calling us to prayer, to penance and to reparation. He has even sent his Mother to Medjugorje to bring us this very message. Always, he looks on us with all the love of his Sacred Heart and his Divine Mercy. He gives us his mother to intercede for us. If indeed the Church is on the cross, we know that resurrection is near, and with resurrection a new springtime.

Thank you for your patience and may the Lord continue to overshadow you with the Spirit as he did our Blessed Mother. Magnificat anima mea dominum.

(Romans 8:28)

Fall 2002

During August I had the privilege with Sr. Briege and some friends of being present when Pope John Paul II dedicated the Shrine of Divine Mercy which is at Lagiemiki on the outskirts of Krakow. The new Shrine is literally a stone's throw from the factory where he worked as a young man. Very touchingly he made reference to this during the dedication of the new Shrine. He said in his address "It is a great mystery of Divine Providence that a young man in clogs who worked at this very place would return here as Pope to dedicate this Shrine."

Obviously, this meant a lot to him personally. It was the culmination of a lifetime's work, which involved the authentication of the devotion of the Divine Mercy, the approval of Sister Faustina's Writings and her canonization as St. Faustina.

Sitting listening to him speak, people experienced the anointing presence of the Holy Spirit and many had difficulty in holding back their tears. He said, "Today, therefore, in this Shrine, I wish solemnly to entrust the world to Divine Mercy. I do so with the burning desire that the message of God's merciful love, proclaimed here through Saint Faustina, may be made known to all the peoples of the earth and fill their hearts with hope. MLW this message radiate from this place to our beloved homeland and go throughout the world …. How greatly today's world needs God's mercy! In every continent, from the depth of human suffering, a cry for mercy seems to rise up. Where hatred and the thirst for revenge dominate, where war brings suffering and death to the innocent, there the grace of mercy is needed in order to settle human minds and hearts and to bring about peace. Wherever respect for life and human dignity are lacking, there is need of God's merciful love, in whose light we see the inexpressible value of every human being. Mercy is needed in order to ensure that every injustice in the world will come to an end in the splendor of truth."

Personally I was deeply moved by the grace of that wonderful

13

day. One could not listen to the Pope speak these words and not have the feeling that a great mystical event was taking place.

Unfortunately, many people in the Church, including many clergy, have adopted a dismissive attitude towards this grace given to the Church and the spiritual movement which it represents. I am convinced that since it was revealed to a woman, that women will be the greatest protagonists of the Divine Mercy. I believe that Magnificat has a significant part to play; in creating an awareness of this spiritual movement. I have always thought that Fr. Harold Cohen was given a special insight and inspiration in the way that he promoted this devotion. We should try to emulate him.

On a final personal note: on the following Monday, two days later, we happened to be in Krakow again and visited the Shrine in the off chance of being able to celebrate the Eucharist at the altar where the Holy Father had said Mass. As it turned out, they allowed me to continue to celebrate the Holy Eucharist every Saturday for the intentions of all of you in Magnificat. "My soul magnifies the Lord."

Spring 2003

When Jesus made His first appearance to the apostles on Easter Sunday, He said to them, "Peace be with you." Then He breathed on them and said, "Receive the Holy Spirit. If you forgive the sins of any they are forgiven; if you retain the sins of any, they are retained." (John 20:19, 22–23) Jesus was proclaiming that the very first fruits of His Resurrection was the forgiveness of sins. He showed them the wounds in His glorified body, and at that moment He imparted to the Church the power to forgive sins.

In His proclamation of the Luminous Mysteries, wonderfully guided by the Holy Spirit, Pope John Paul II has placed at the center the proclamation of the Kingdom and the call to conversion. The call is a perennial voice, echoing down the centuries of the church. It is by Jesus Himself in this central ministry of reconciliation. At the heart of this ministry of the Church is the celebration of the Sacrament of Reconciliation.

Today unfortunately, many people have gotten out of the habit of going to confession. This is due to a number of factors. Firstly, the amazing tolerance for sin and wickedness which we find in modern society; as well as the widespread view, even among Catholics, that everyone goes to heaven in the end anyway. The second reason for the fall off in the ministry of reconciliation is the failure of priests to call people to repentance. This I believe is due to the fact that we priests do not ourselves make good penitents. What started out being a renewal of the sacrament has turned out to be almost an abolition of it.

Magnificat would be doing a great favor to the Church by impressing upon women, especially young mothers, the need for personal repentance and reconciliation and the equally great need to teach their children about repentance, especially by their example. It has been my observation after long years in the priestly ministry that there is no therapy that even comes near to what people experience when they make a good confession. There we meet the

15

merciful Jesus who forgives our sins and lifts from our shoulders the yoke of pain and guilt. Amen.

Fr. Kevin Scallon, C. M.

Winter 2004

Pope John Paul II, with his unerring discernment concerning the needs of the Church, has called for a special 'Year of the Holy Eucharist' from October 2004 to October 2005. The Pope, as he always does, has listened to the voice of the Holy Spirit and has observed how the Spirit is moving in the hearts of faithful people everywhere.

As you may know, there is a vein of theological thought which says that the Eucharist is supposed to be eaten, not looked at or prayed to. Cardinal Ratzinger has commented on this by pointing out that reverence for the real presence of Christ in the Eucharist goes back to the early Church and not only is Eucharistic devotion orthodox, it is also something to be promoted throughout the Church. It was in response to this movement of the Spirit that the Pope called the whole Church to a deeper faith and more reverent devotion to the Eucharist.

I know that you and all the members of Magnificat have been listening to this invitation of the Spirit. Please continue to promote this unique devotion. Do not worry that you cannot persuade your local pastors to allow exposition of the Blessed Sacrament. This has been a problem in some places. Just remember that the Blessed Sacrament is in every Catholic Church and that Jesus is always there waiting for us to come to Him.

I have always been struck by the prayer which the angel taught the children of Fatima. I believe that it is more relevant now than ever, especially the reference to the need for reparation for all the "outrages, sacrileges and indifference" by which Christ is offended in the Eucharist. We should pray this prayer often:

"Most Holy Trinity, Father, Son and Holy Spirit, I adore You profoundly and I offer You the most precious Body, Blood, Soul and divinity of Jesus Christ, present in all the tabernacles of the world, in reparation for the outrages, sacrileges and indifference with which He Himself is offended. And through the infinite merits of His most

Sacred Heart, and the Immaculate Heart of Mary, I beg You the conversion of poor sinners."

Fr. Kevin Scallon, C. M.

Fall 2003

My friend Fr. Francis Martin told me recently that he believes that the Lord has handed everything over to Mary and that if we need anything from God, it is to Mary we should go. My recent visit to Medjugorje really confirmed that thought. It is indeed a place of extraordinary grace for the church and for the whole world. There you sense Jesus pleading with us to listen to the promise of His Mercy. You sense Him saying, "and if you will not listen to me, please listen to my Mother." She really does want to give us everything; we just will not listen.

The hidden decay in the church is now there for all to see, thirty years a-festering. It is now time for radical conversion and change. Pray that the Lord will raise up great pastors in the church. I think this has already begun in Boston and in other places.

I look forward to meeting you at our Conference in September. Let us all pray earnestly that it will turn out to be a wonderful grace for the women of the Church. As the women are, so also is the Church.

In the Love of Christ,
Rev. Kevin J. Scallon, C.M.

"We pray that the perennial grace of Pentecost, which is the Church, will be in the hearts of everyone in Magnificat and will indeed lead us to "a renewed incentive to prayer, holiness, communion and proclamation."

Last Advent I heard a lady in a Catholic bookstore ask if they sold the Christmas nail. She was directed where to find it. I could not help asking her what the Christmas nail was. She explained to me, that where she came from in Eastern Europe they had the custom of hanging a long iron nail on a bough of the Christmas tree near to the trunk. It was to remind the family that there was another tree associated with Christ, the tree of the cross.

Recently I was invited to view Mel Gibson's movie "The Passion of Christ." It was a stunning unforgettable experience. It is a work of power and excellence, never before achieved in the art of the cinema. Nothing is held back from the agony of Christ in the garden to his death on the cross. For Mel Gibson there is no well-coiffed Christ, no designer crown of thorns, but only the brutish pagan barbarism which was visited on the Son of God. His enemies are portrayed for what they were, men whose ears had long since stopped hearing the word of God and who felt threatened by the truth coming from the lips of Jesus. There is nothing in the movie that is not found in the gospels. It is violently anti-violence teaching us that every whip wielded, every bullet fired, every bomb dropped afflicts the body of Christ with deep wounds. Mary is beautifully portrayed by a wonderful actress. She follows her son everywhere; she reaches out to him, to Peter, to Magdalene and to the beloved disciple. She wipes his blood off the pavement with linen cloths; she stands at the cross with John. This movie is Marian in a wonderfully inspired way. Here we see a woman who draws strength from knowing who she is and who her son is. Her "be it done" is in her eyes at every moment. Jim Caviezel will probably not get the academy award for best actor, but his portrayal of the suffering Christ is nothing short of brilliant. It is inspired, anointed by the Holy Spirit, profoundly Eucharistic.

Those who have seen "The Passion of Christ" love it and are bowled over by it: those who have not seen it hate it. When it comes out, go and see it. Until then, tell people about it. You will be doing a service to God.

May the tree of Christmas always remind you that the Child Jesus born for us now is Christ the Lord who was nailed to the tree of the cross and died to save us from sin and death. May you and all your loved ones have a peaceful and blessed Christmas season and all of God's blessings in the New Year.

Fr. Kevin Scallon, C. M.

Spring 2004

When I was a boy at primary school, every year the teachers tried to persuade us *to make the Stations of the Cross* each day during Lent. Many of us would do it. I used to run to the church after school and almost literally run around the stations and then run home. Apart from the dialogue with Jesus and Mary—Simon of Cyrene, Veronica and the poor women of Jerusalem heard little from me in those days. But, however badly we may do something, which is in itself good; grace will always be at work. From that time in my childhood, I have always had a great love for this devotion.

The *Stations of the Cross* is a devotion that goes back to the fourteenth century when it was introduced by the Franciscan Father who also gave us the Christmas crib and devotion to the *Most Blessed Sacrament reserved in the tabernacle.* The *Stations of the Cross* commemorate the journey of Jesus and his death on the cross. They are prayed by moving from one station to the next while praying and meditating on each scene of the passion. Nowadays, I often pray the Stations by saying a decade of the *Divine Mercy Chaplet* at each station; but everyone will have their own way of doing the *Stations of the Cross.* Anyone unfamiliar with this devotion should perhaps get a little prayer book as a help at the beginning.

I think it is a great pity that this lovely devotional practice so suited to the season of Lent has almost died out. Mel Gibson has given us a powerful meditation of the *Passion* to help us. There is also an excellent recording by Dana and an Irish priest, whose name escapes me at the moment.

I pray that *Magnificat* will be instrumental in renewing this beautiful devotional practice in the Church. *We adore You, O Christ, and we praise You; because by your cross You have redeemed the world.*

[Editor's note: Modesty prevents Fr. Kevin from naming the Irish priest who made the above-mentioned recording with Dana. We, on the other hand, are quite free to tell you that it's none other than himself, as the Irish would say.]

Summer 2004

Croist Linn (Christ with us) *is the name of a community of lay people in Ireland whom I have been directing for the last twenty years. It is made up of people from a broad spectrum of Irish life. The latest member was an I.R.S (Irish Republican Army) bomber who got baptized in the Spirit while spending fourteen years in England as a guest of Her Majesty Queen Elizabeth II. He is about to begin his studies for the priesthood, so pray for him. When I started with this little community, I became convinced that I should stand back to see how the Holy Spirit would lead them and which charisms he would impart to them. What I observed was most interesting. The first charism and the most powerful was their devotion to the Eucharist, both in their attendance at daily Mass and their devotion to the Blessed Sacrament. Most of them had been involved in prayer meetings; so the use of charismatic gifts was quite familiar to them.*

After that, I could see how strong was their devotion to Mary and how easily they related to her as their mother. Somehow, and without any prompting from me, they were drawn to make the consecration and entrustment to Our Blessed Lady as taught in the writings of St. Louis de Montfort, especially his little book, "The True Devotion." But what surprised me more than anything else were the extraordinary graces of mystical prayer which the Lord gave them. They have received many other gifts such as peace, harmony, and hospitality and, of course, a genuine love for each other.

I mention these things because I have observed the same pattern of development in other communities, notably the "Emmanuel" and the "Beatitude" communities in France, as well as others in Italy. I suppose we ought not to be surprised at this since these are the foundational charisms of Catholic piety and spirituality. Through the Holy Spirit, the Eucharist gives us the Church and the Church gives us the Eucharist. The Father give Mary to Jesus as His Mother and Jesus give Mary to us as our mother. Through our contemplation of the Trinity with Mary we grow in holiness of life.

Pope John Paul II has designated the year 2004–2005 as a special year of the Eucharist. We pray that church leaders will respond to this prophetic instinct of the Holy Father. We of Magnificat should take the Pope's call very seriously indeed. We should keep before us the words of the Holy Father spoken on Pentecost Sunday: "I greet in a special way the members of the Renewal in the Spirit, one of the various branches of the great family of the Catholic Charismatic Movement. Thanks to the Charismatic, a multitude of Christians, men and women, young people and adults have rediscovered Pentecost as a living reality in their daily lives. I hope that the spirituality of Pentecost will spread in the Church as a renewed incentive to prayer, holiness, communion and proclamation."

He then goes on to say this about devotion to the Holy Eucharist: "In this regard, I encourage the initiative known as "Burning Bush," promoted by Renewal in the Spirit. This involves perpetual adoration, day and night, before the Blessed Sacrament; it is an invitation to the faithful to 'return to the Upper Room,' so that, united in contemplation of the Eucharistic Mystery, they may intercede for full Christian unity and for the conversion of sinners. I warmly hope that this initiative will lead many to rediscover the gifts of the Spirit, whose original source is Pentecost."

We pray that the perennial grace of Pentecost, which is the Church, will be in the hearts of everyone in Magnificat and will indeed lead us to "a renewed incentive to prayer, holiness, communion and proclamation."

Spring 2005

At the Second Vatican Council, the Holy Spirit inspired the council Fathers to remind us that the Church is made up of all the baptized, that it is a Church of the laity as well as the hierarchy. I suppose we always knew this even though "The Church" in former times was synonymous with the Bishops and the clergy. In the last twenty years traveling around with Sr. Briege, it is quite remarkable to observe how this transformation has been taking place. This has not been happening because of any real conscious activity on the part of the church hierarchy, but simply as a result of the work of the Holy Spirit. In many places in the world where we have traveled, most of the really successful events that have taken place in connection with our ministry have originated and have been organized by lay men and women in love with the church. These people who themselves have had a personal encounter with the risen Christ. They are people of unimpeachable orthodoxy, men and women of prayer, who are well versed in the scriptures and the teachings of the Church, and who engage daily in a life of prayer.

Sr. Briege and myself are leaving to give two priest retreats in Brazil on February 27th. What was remarkable about our last visit to Brazil was our meeting with a young man called Moyses who in his late twenties founded a lay community called Shalom. This community under the leadership of Moyses organized a priest retreat in Fortaleza for several hundred priests. They did this, of course, in consultation with the local Bishop, but the idea had come from him, and they organized it lovingly and efficiently. I don't know how many of the priests were touched by what Sr. Briege and I had said to them, but I do know that their hearts were deeply moved by the love and the welcome which they received from these lay servants of Christ.

On our recent visit to Indonesia we encountered the same phenomenon with the added feature of a financial commitment so generous that the priests attending did so without having to pay for their airfare or their accommodations. At the end of September we are directing a priests' retreat in the town of Ars in France, the home of St. John Vianney, the famous Cure d'Ars. This retreat also is being sponsored and organized primarily by the Community of the Beatitudes.

At the moment I am reading the revelations of "Anna," who describes herself as a "Lay Apostle" and a secular Franciscan. Anna is living in Ireland, although she was born in the United States. She is married with six children. Her writings could only be described as Theresian in their spirit, depth and beauty. She is a woman who is extremely conscious of her need to be in obedience to the official Church and she does nothing and says nothing without receiving direction and permission from her local Bishop. If I were to pick someone for such a privileged role, I probably would never have looked twice in her direction. The Lord knew her heart and is using her in extraordinary ways. There are many others which I could describe if I had the time, but there is no doubt that the Lord is moving very powerfully in the Church and in the hearts of His people.

A significant initiative towards the women of the Church known as "Magnificat," to which you all belong, is itself something initiated by lay women who love the Lord, who love the Church, and have a vision for the role of women. Magnificat, of course, is in the mainstream of this golden river flowing through the Church spreading the light of the Spirit and the refreshment of God's grace in every direction. As individual members we should never be disappointed at the extent to which divine providence has circumscribed our lives. The Lord works through littleness and hiddenness and every thought and prayer and pain that is offered to Him reaches to the end of the earth bringing salvation to many.

Fr. Kevin Scallon, C. M.

Summer 2005

My friend Fr. Neal McDermott tells me that he has a homily on "Catholic beliefs that were not abolished at Vatican II." I have not heard his homily, but I could sure preach one of my own. Some time ago in a conversation the subject of confession came up and a lady said to me, "Confession! Do we still do that? I thought that it had been done away with at Vatican II." Tragically, it is true that most people today do not go to confession (Sacrament of Reconciliation). The effects of this are to be seen everywhere and in every facet of our lives—the lack of prayer and reverence for God, profanity, lack of respect for people, for holy places and for holy things, immodesty, intemperance, disobedience within families, etc., etc.

I know a young woman who married a divorced man. She said that because of her age, she could not wait for the annulment to come through. She wanted a Church wedding, which an "understanding" priest friend was willing to provide. It was all explained because she felt it was the right thing to do, since they really did love each other. Was this wrong? Yes, it was. Was the priest wrong? Very definitely, he was wrong. Marriage is still marriage. It is one of the Sacraments of the Church. Adultery is still adultery, no matter how you dress it up or what lovely words are used to describe it. I am completely amazed at how many people, who live in invalid unions or are cohabiting, regularly go to receive the Holy Eucharist similarly with people who have lapsed from the practice of the Catholic faith. Does anything go now? Or does it not matter anymore. Are conscientious Catholics just old fusspots? Regrettably, people are making up their own rules or simply abolishing all rules. In an age of abortion and euthanasia, where a judge from the bench can pronounce it legal to starve a young woman to death, I guess we ought not to be surprised by anything. Witnessing to the truth is just getting more and more difficult—but not impossible.

We in Magnificat are called to pray for our beloved Church, to know her teaching and to live them through the grace of the Sacraments in the power of the Holy Spirit. May we be lights in the midst of darkness, inspiring and helping others to do the same.

Winter 2005

E arlier this year I decided with Sr. Briege to take my brother and his wife to the Shrine of the Divine Mercy in Poland. This was as a result of a promise I had made to him some time ago. About a week prior to our departure I had the inspiration to call Anne the lay apostle, whose writings many of you have been reading. I wasn't sure if she would want to go or not, but it proved to be a confirmation of something that she had been feeling herself. So we traveled via Frankfurt to Poland on October 17th. We were met by a good friend Fr. Tadeusz who housed us and drove us and generally treated us like royalty for the duration of our time.

The Diving Mercy Shrine is on the grounds of the convent where St. Faustina had her revelation concerning the Divine Mercy. This is a very special place made more so by the new Basilica, the opening of which we attended when Pope John Paul II consecrated it in 2002. To go there is to be in the presence of the merciful Christ. You sense that immediately; you know that you're in an atmosphere of great grand and blessing. The day before we went to the Shrine we made a little pilgrimage to the Shrine of Our Lady of Czestochowa. For Polish people, of course, this is the premier Shrine of Our Lady and there is always a constant flow of pilgrims who pray and attend the Eucharist in that holy place.

On the second day of our pilgrimage to the Divine Mercy Shrine in Cracow-Lagiewniki, I was privileged to celebrate the Eucharist at the altar in the convent chapel. During the Mass I became conscious of the need to pray for Magnificat throughout the world; that God would continue to bless this beautiful movement within the Church and through it to bring many people to holiness of life. In the afternoon of that day we visited the convent, thanks to the good graces of Fr. Tadeusz who knew the Mother Superior very well. Anne was with us and we decided to introduce her to Mother Mary Lukasza. We explained to the sisters who Anne was and spoke about the message and her writings. She then began to tell the sisters about her experience with the Lord and most recently with St. Faustina herself. When she mentioned that her mission was to spread the message of Jesus Christ the Returning King, Mother Mary Lukasza told her about something very strange that had happened to her the day before. She explained that on her feast day an artist friend of hers had presented her with a painting, which he had told her would be a painting of her patron saint. But when he gave her the painting, he explained that it was a painting of Christ the King. She immediately went off to fetch the painting and when we saw it, all of us in the room were amazed and recognized immediately that this painting was to be the authentic image for the apostolate representing Jesus Christ the Returning King. It was obvious that Mother Lukasza had the exact same sense, because she immediately presented the painting to Anne telling her that she was certain that it was really meant for her. We all felt that we were present at a moment of great significance which we will look back on with great gratitude.

In the days before coming to Poland, Anne shared with me that she had received messages from St. Faustina who told her that the revelation of Divine Mercy and of Christ the Returning King were intimately connected which is why she was so amazed to receive the painting—almost, you might say, from the hands of St. Faustina herself. St. Faustina had told her that the Divine Mercy devotion was more for these times in which we live than for any other time in the past.

For myself, I feel very convicted of the authenticity of the messages which Anne has shared with the world through her writings and I look forward to the book which she has written and which I understand will be published before the end of this year. The great consolation I take form all of this is that the Lord is visibly purifying the world and the Church, and that, please God, all of us will live to see the new springtime which will emerge from these times of purification.

Totus Tuus

The de Montfort Consecration to Mary the Mother of God

The Consecration to the Blessed Virgin Mary according to the teaching and spirituality of St. Louis de Montfort is quite unique in Catholic spirituality. It is, therefore, very important that we have a clear understanding of what is involved in making this consecration. It is not like being enrolled in the Association of the Miraculous Medal or the Sacred Heart Confraternity or the Holy Name Society. These are loose associations that carry no real obligation with them. We can join and leave them as we wish. The de Montfort Consecration however is of a totally different character because it involves a solemn and lasting dedication and entrustment of our lives and we have to Jesus through the Blessed Virgin Mary. So it is more than just a promise. It is a solemn consecration which, when properly prepared for and solemnly made, becomes irrevocable.

When we understand the nature of this entrustment, we realize that we are handing over to the Blessed Virgin Mary all our natural and spiritual goods. We should understand clearly that our Blessed Lady takes possession of these spiritual goods and applies them where she thinks fit. This act of total consecration to Mary means that we place in her hands all our good deeds, past, present and to come, so as to do with them as she wishes. The merits obtained from our good works are taken care of and perfected by our Blessed Mother in order to make them acceptable to Jesus her Son. In this act of consecration we give up even our very selves; we give away ownership of our body and soul and of all our spiritual and material possessions. We even abandon our right to dispose of the value of any of our good deeds. This means that we must entrust to our Blessed Mother all that we have, so that she may care for us in the same way that she cared for the needs of Jesus her Son. This means that we can never demand anything back from her and that is serving Mary as her total possession. We rely on her for everything. We entrust ourselves in all circumstances to be guided by her wisdom and we trust that she will distribute all our good works in the most perfect manner. And even after making this consecration we forget about it, which please God we would never do, Mary still remains faithful and will continue to accept our total servitude. She will continue to use us to overcome the powers of darkness in the world.

Because of the nature of this consecration and its seriousness, it is important that those intending to make it prepare themselves well. St. Louis de Montfort himself recommends a month-long preparation for this consecration.

It should be made during or after Mass, on one or other of the feasts of the Blessed Mother. It is good to write out the act of total consecration so that it includes your own name and keep it in your bible or some suitable place. This paper becomes a deed of ownership by Our Blessed Lady. Having made this consecration in this solemn way, it should be repeated solemnly every year, and privately as often as we wish.

On a personal note, I made the de Montfort consecration before I was ordained a deacon and I regard it as one of the great well-springs of divine grace in my life and in my priestly ministry. More and more I understand it as placing myself in Mary's hands, like a tool in the hands of a tradesman. Having given myself to her, she has repaid me many times over. She knows far better than I how I should serve her Son Jesus.

Some people have misgivings about making such a complete consecration to the Mother of God and find it difficult to enter into the spirituality of this consecration. Anyone who has such difficulties would be advised not to make such a consecration until their problems have been resolved through prayer and study. However, take comfort from the fact that the greatest servant of God whose life and ministry has been such a blessing to the Church, namely, Pope John Paul II, did make this consecration and proclaimed it to the whole Church and the whole world in his motto Totus Tuus. These words are taken from an antiphon in the Little Office of Our Blessed Lady: "I am all yours, O Holy and Immaculate One, and all that I have in time and eternity is yours." St. Louis de Montfort recommended praying this antiphon very frequently. So I would therefore recommend that everyone in Magnificat read the writings of St. Louis de Montfort, especially, "The True Devotion to the Blessed Virgin Mary" and "The Secret of Mary."

I greet you all in the heart of Jesus, our crucified Savior, and I pray for all of you especially at the Masses I offer for Magnificat every Saturday. I wish you every blessing, especially during this Easter season. May you be bathed in the saving blood of our Savior Jesus and rejoice in His glorious Resurrection.

Rev. Kevin J. Scallon, C.M

"For the sake of His sorrowful passion, have mercy on us and on the whole world."

Divine Mercy prayer

Summer 2006

For quite some time there has been a strong negative reaction by many, including clergy, to traditional popular devotions. One that immediately springs to mind is the Chaplet of Divine Mercy.

The disparagement of such devotions would seem to indicate a failure to understand what God is doing through these popular movements of Catholic piety and prayer. When Jesus promised the Holy Spirit, Who would "teach you all things" (Jn. 14:26), He surely meant to include methods of praying to draw us more and more into the life of the Trinity. Such is the love of the Father that He sent His Son among us to save us from sin and death (Jn. 3:16). It is clearly the will of the Father that we should come to know His Son Jesus: "He who sees Me sees the Father" (Jn. 14:9). It seems to me that the raison d'etre of evangelization and pastoral care is to bring about a deep mystical union of every baptized person with Jesus Christ and through Him with the Trinity. We may often forget this, but God does not forget and is always providing us with ways and means to bring about this union. If we do not know how to pray, the Holy Spirit steps in to teach us and to pray on our behalf. (cf. Rom. 8:26)

Hence it is that down the centuries of the Church's history, we witnessed the emergence of many forms of popular devotion. Pilgrimage is one of the oldest and is certainly one of the most enduring. The idea of setting out on a journey to a holy place (originally the Holy Land) in a spirit of prayer and fasting in order to obtain some special grace or favor is as old as the Church. To this day the followers of Jesus still do this. Supreme of all of these devotions is that to the Presence of Jesus in the Most Blessed Sacrament, made popular by St. Francis of Assisi. St. Francis is also credited with giving the Church the Stations of the Cross, a devotion sadly neglected in our modern Church. The Rosary given by our Blessed Mother to St. Dominic is perhaps the most widely practiced of all. Then there are the multitudes of prayers and novenas to Mary and to the Saints and the Angels: too many to be enumerated, but all never-the-less loved and practiced by generations of simple, faithful people.

There can be no doubt that all these forms of prayer are the work of the Spirit of Jesus Who sits at the right hand of the Father "always living to make intercession for us" (Heb. 7:25). If more learned or enlightened fold look askance at such pious practices, they really ought not to do so. We should always remind ourselves that the simpler and more humble our way of prayer, the more pleasing it is in the sight of God. Some of the deepest contemplatives I have ever met are people who never even read a page of St. Theresa, never mind St. John of the Cross; but they love the Miraculous Medal Novena, they love going to Lourdes, or making the Stations of the Cross during Lent. These devotions were and are mystical paths followed by generations of Catholics who lived lives of repentance open to the grace of the Holy Spirit: people whose banners might read "God bless the Sacred Heart" The local pastor may not have approved, but I dare say the Heavenly Father was delighted, tickled pink, over the moon.

Father Kevin

The Rosary: A Walk to Emmaus

When I was a boy I used to watch my father stooped across a chair as we all knelt saying the family rosary: my mother beside him. Somehow, you expect your mother to be a person of prayer, but there is something powerfully impressive about watching your father at prayer. It is an image that has stayed with me all my life and to this day, has been the best sermon I have ever "heard" on prayer.

The greatness of the rosary lies in its power to help us walk in the footsteps of Jesus. It draws us into those eternal moments in the life of Christ. In each mystery we gaze, as through a window, to contemplate with Mary, the life and mysteries of her Son. As at all her great shrines, Mary is never concerned to draw her children to herself but to her Son. We recite the Hail Mary's and gaze on Jesus who allows us to be with him at each moment from the Annunciation to the Crowning of his Mother as Queen. The rosary, like the cycle of the liturgical year, follows Jesus from the events of his young life—the Joyful Mysteries; through his passion and death—the Sorrowful Mysteries, culminating in his Glorious Resurrection, Pentecost and the final Glorification of Mary—"The woman clothed with the sun" (Rev. 12:1). For simplicity and depth it would be hard to imagine a more perfect prayer. As we finger the beads and recite the Hail Mary's, the words of scripture pass before our mind and we drink from "the spring of living water welling up to eternal life" (Jn 4: 14) and "our hearts burn within us." (Lk 24:32)

Some years ago, I called on a friend of mine. His wife told me that he was in the den. What she didn't tell me was that he was with his ten-year-old son teaching him how to pray the rosary. I would be willing to be that little boy will never forget how to pray the rosary as long as he lives. Sadly, there are so many today who do not know how to say this wonderful prayer. Dare we hope that Fr. Peyton's great slogan could be heard once again and that families might begin to pray the rosary once more. The rosary is everyone's prayer. Princes and presidents, rich and poor, young and old, saints and sinners, find in it a way of praying that is simple and yet profound. Our Blessed Mother loves this prayer. The church has set aside this month of October as the month of the Holy Rosary. St. Padre Pio said that "the Rosary is like a great sword that Mary puts into the hands of her children to defend themselves against the evil one." Very many people, including myself, have found this to be true. Our Blessed Mother does help us in moments of spiritual combat. The powers of darkness fear her and flee from her presence.

Everyone has a personal approach to this prayer. I like to say it in a quiet place on my own. I keep a rosary in my right-hand pocket and I pray it as I stand in line or wait for planes or trains or whatever it may be. Families should pray it in the home with an image of Mary, a lighted candle and with each member being asked to do their part. German-speaking peoples have the custom of adding a phrase after the name of "Jesus" in the first half of the Hail Mary. This phrase helps to keep in mind the theme of each decade, for example: ... thy womb Jesus, to whom you Mary give birth ... thy womb Jesus, who was crucified for us ... "or thy womb Jesus, who crowned you Virgin Mary in heaven ..." Personally, I have found this an extremely helpful way of keeping my mind at rest while meditating on each mystery. And, of course, the rosary has a definite therapeutic effect. When you find prayer difficult, the rosary will help you; it will pray for you; it will quiet your distracted mind or troubled soul and bring you to calmness and serenity. In fact, according to a study in the British Medical Journal, reciting the rosary could improve your cardiovascular well being. Seemingly it has the effect of synchronizing respiratory and cardiac rhythms; which, as everyone knows, could only be good for you.

Fr. Kevin Scallon, C. M.

"The rosary is everyone's prayer."

The Lord, the giver of life

Pope Benedict recently referred to the Holy Spirit as the "soul of our souls," echoing, no doubt, the famous prayer of Cardinal Mercier, "O Holy Spirit, soul of my soul, I adore you, etc."

The Holy Spirit, the third person of the Trinity, is the personification of the love that passes from the Father to the Son and from the Son to the Father for all eternity. Through our baptism, we are brought into this cycle of love by the power of the Holy Spirit.

Each day at Mass the priest stretching out his hands over the bread and wine prays,

"Father we bring you these gifts. We ask you to make them holy by the power of your Spirit, that they may become the Body and Blood of your Son, our Lord Jesus Christ." Even the Eucharist is conferred by the power of the Holy Spirit. This is true of all sacraments. Christ is present in every word proclaimed and in every sacrament ministered by the power of the Holy Spirit. Indeed, everything that happens in the Church is the work of the Spirit. The Holy Spirit acts in and through the Father and the Son, three persons, one God. So it is with the baptized soul, the Holy Spirit is indeed the soul of our soul.

Many have experienced what has come to be known as the baptism in the Holy Spirit. We all remember the moment when something happened to us. This is the work of the Holy Spirit. For me it happened sitting alone before the Blessed Sacrament in a rectory chapel at 9:30 on a Friday morning. The Holy Spirit did to me was to make me aware as never before of the person of Jesus. It was a momentary experience that changed my life and my priestly ministry.

Pope John Paul II referred to the baptism in the Holy Spirit as "a personal encounter with the risen Christ." That indeed is what it is. Christ becomes a living reality to us and this reality changes us forever. It is a mind-illuminating, eye-opening, mystical experience which enables us to see and understand what our life in Christ really means. We experience the power of the Holy Spirit; we experience the person of Jesus as Lord and Savior; we experience our membership in the Body of Christ, the Church; we experience the reality of Christ in the Eucharist and in the Blessed Sacrament; we experience Jesus in each of the Sacraments. In addition to all this, we become aware of many of the gifts and fruits of the Holy Spirit in our lives; above all love, but also joy, peace, patience, kindness, goodness, trustfulness, gentleness and self-control. [Galatians 5] The work of the Holy Spirit is to draw us more and more into the life of the Triune God where we experience the love of the Father, the mercy of Jesus and the power of the Holy Spirit.

An Orthodox bishop wrote this about the Holy Spirit. He says,

"Without the Holy Spirit, God is far away,
Christ stays in the past,
the Gospel is a dead letter,
the Church is simply an organization,
authority a matter of domination,
mission a matter of propaganda,
the liturgy no more than an evocation,
Christian living a slave morality.
But in the Holy Spirit:
the cosmos is resurrected and groans
with the birth pangs of the kingdom,
the risen Christ is there,
the Gospel is the power of life,
the Church shows forth the life of the Trinity,
authority is a liberating service,
mission is a Pentecost,
the liturgy is both memorial and anticipation,
human action is deified."

I write these few words as a meditation to help you prepare for the upcoming conference in March. May the Lord bless you this Christmas and throughout the coming year.

Rev. Kevin J. Scallon, C.M.

Brother Elia

Brother Elia lives in Calvi somewhere in Umbria, Italy. He is now in his early forties. As a boy, strange things began to happen to him during Lent. He would lose his appetite and wind up not eating for the entire six weeks of Lent. He became so weak and so debilitated that his parents brought him to see the doctor who diagnosed that he was under-nourished, but could offer no explanation as to why he didn't eat. It was only during Lent that this happened. When Holy Saturday would come he would return to his normal eating pattern. It wasn't until he became a teenager and the marks of Christ's Passion began to appear on his body that it suddenly dawned on his parents and the doctors that this was something quite out of the ordinary. On one occasion he told his mother that he could see angels; of course, his mother didn't believe him.

Many other things happened around this young man. He was very devout and very prayerful. In his twenties he took a job as postman in Milan. One day, when he was delivering a package to the Franciscan friary, he had a very profound experience of the presence of God. As a result of this experience, he joined the Franciscan community there; but when the experience of the Passion began to happen to him, they more or less decided that his vocation lay somewhere else. In due course he left the Franciscan community and was led by the Lord to found a community of brothers "The Apostles of God." Later on he acquired an old Franciscan friary, which at one time had been visited by Francis himself and from which he sent out his friars to North Africa where they were subsequently martyred. Brother Elia undertook the refurbishment of this old building and is living there now with his embryonic community of brothers. He feels that his vocation is to reach out to the young people of the world, particularly those who are in the most desolate situations. He is already building an extension to the friary and has plans to build a great basilica in honor of the apostles. He believes that great healing can come to young people through their contact with nature and even with farm animals, so he has pigs, goats, poultry and horses.

Sr. Briege and I met him at the beginning of Holy Week and spent a good part of a day with him. We celebrated the Eucharist and afterwards he talked to us about many things. When we told him we were ministering to priests, he prayed for us and urged us to continue this very important work. He is very concerned about the weakness and the lack of fortitude that seems to exist amongst bishops and priests. He told us to warn priests that they are first and foremost shepherds of the flock and that they should avoid anything like careerism in their priestly life. He had many other things to say, which I haven't time to recount here.

Each year during Holy Week the wounds of Christ appear fully in his body, including the wounds of the thorns on his head. He suffers greatly and told us how lonely and how desolate this experience is for him. I spoke to him about Ann the Apostle, whom you will be familiar with from the movement of Direction for Our Times. He said, "I know Ann; I know this woman in prayer." This astonished us. He also mentioned that he knew of Father Sudatz and that he needed the support of our prayers.

Brother Elia has a little shop at his friary and when I visited, my eyes fell on a beautiful wooden crucifix which I was determined to purchase for myself. I did this and I asked the girl to bring it to Brother Elia so that he would pray over it and place it on the altar in his little chapel. To my surprise, he came back to me with the crucifix and gave it to me with a knowing look and a smile. I thought to myself, now this is a real personal treasure for me and a great souvenir of my visit to Brother Elia. When I got to Rome and took out the crucifix to look at it, I clearly heard the Lord saying to me; "This crucifix is not for you, but is to be given to Ann." I immediately tried to deny this word and even asked Sr. Briege if maybe I was talking to myself. But I think we both knew that it was really a clear directive from the Lord. When I came home to Ireland and met Ann, she told me that she had been looking for a nice crucifix for their oratory and that she had been unable to choose one from the many she had seen in various places. When I told her about my crucifix, she was astounded and when she saw it, she immediately recognized it as the one the Lord had intended for her.

Not many people know about Brother Elia yet, but I thought you might be interested in hearing about him because I think the Lord will bring him before the whole Church very soon. He has a website which you might want to visit: www.fraelia.com. Brother Elia is another example of how the Lord is raising up great saints and holy people to renew the face of the Church. Pray for him, that the Lord's perfect plan for his life may be protected and fulfilled in every way. I pray that the Holy Spirit will visit you with His many gifts, as you prepare for His coming at Pentecost. God bless you all.

Fr. Kevin Scallon, C.M.

"Singing Priest"

Not long ago Sr. Briege and I went to conduct a priests' retreat in Lithuania where the Church was persecuted and the priests suffered greatly under the Communist regime. They were without their own Bishops for several decades. Thankfully, since the fall of the old atheistic government, they now have their own Bishops and a brand new seminary which is producing crops of fine young priests. One of the seminarians came to talk to me about his studies. During our conversation he said, "Would you like me to tell you how I got my vocation?"

I love vocation stories, so I said, "Sure, I'd love to hear it." He told me a remarkable story of how the Lord called him to the priesthood.

When he finished I said, "Would you like to write this down so that I may be able to use it sometime in the future?" He agreed. This is what he wrote:

> I am a 33-year-old deacon from Vilnius (Lithuania). In 2000—a milestone in my life—I had just finished my Bachelor's degree at the Music Academy of Lithuania and had been accepted to study Opera in a Master's program. I felt very content, because there was plenty of work. For example, I produced different entertainment shows, was a master of ceremonies, as well as a singer and drama teacher. During this time there was no lack of money or women either.

> On the 15 of September that year, I participated in my friends' wedding. The beautiful voice of the priest made the wedding ceremony a glorious event. In the middle of the ceremony I heard someone call me by name. I turned around, but couldn't see anybody. I thought to myself that I had just overheard something and continued to watch the wedding. Then I heard it again: "Povilas, Povilas!" I

turned around, but again I could see nobody calling me. I looked at the people standing beside me, but they didn't look as if they had heard anything. The situation seemed strange to me, but I didn't pay much attention to it. When I heard somebody calling my name for the third time, I somehow knew that it was God's voice. He told me: "Your life belongs to Me."

I soon forgot about this event, but two weeks later He spoke to me again. Just as the first time, I heard His voice not in my head or heart, but audibly, just as I can hear different noises like wind blowing or people talking. God reminded me that my life belongs to Him and showed me the direction I was to take in my life. Even though I was talking to God, I didn't want to agree with His plan as I felt content with my life and didn't have any desire to change it. God didn't argue with me. He just reminded me again that my life belonged to Him. A conversation like that reoccurred a couple more times during the next two weeks, but I wasn't about to give in.

During that year the quality of my singing was rapidly improving and there was hope to make a successful career as a singer. However at the end of November I started having problems with my voice and singing became more and more difficult. On the eve of each concert I sang in, the Lord would ask me to answer His calling. I would promise to think about His plan if He healed my voice for the next day's performance. The next day after the successful performance I would rudely tell God that I didn't want to hear about His calling. The sickness would then come back.

I am ashamed now to admit that during that year my behavior toward God was obnoxious. In fact, I was ruder than I have been with anybody else before—even compared to those who wished me ill. I continued being rude and kept trying His patience until January 12, a day before a special concert given in memory of the events that occurred on the 13th of January in 1991 (the USSR army attacked the Republic of Lithuania). I was invited to sing live on national TV. That morning during the rehearsal I completely lost my voice. My doctor refused to continue treatment admitting that she couldn't detect the source of my sickness and that my body wasn't reacting to any medication.

The next two weeks were the hardest in my life. I felt as though I had lost the foundation of my life. I was crying out to God, but He was silent. Finally I understood that God used this situation to talk to me as the way to draw my attention.

Then I promised God that if He gave me my voice back, I would seriously consider His plan; however, if I decided not to follow it, He would stop pursuing me. His agreement to this pact was the last time that I audibly heard God's voice. While fulfilling my promise to God, I started seriously considering becoming a priest. At the same time I was secretly hoping that I would conclude that this was not my calling. Then I started reading the Bible, which I hadn't done before. I was shocked to read about the callings of both the prophet Samuel and the apostle Paul. In some ways these were similar to mine. Because of these similarities, for three years I was embarrassed to tell my story to anybody except my parents.

As the end of January 2001, almost a year later, I woke up one day with the knowledge in my heart that God had changed my heart and that His calling had become the way of my life. I immediately shared about that with my parents and my girlfriend whom I then loved.

I thought that I was happy before God called me to Himself. But I never even imagined that it is possible to be so happy when you place your life into the hands of God. Sometimes people who have heard my story ask me, why God chose such an unusual way to communicate with me. While praying about it I understood that it wasn't because

I was better than others, but simply because I was "deaf" to all of His other invitations. God used what it took to draw my attention and to help me hear His voice when I was "deaf."

Thank You, Lord, for calling and thank You for Your unlimited love and patience with Your once "deaf" child.

This excerpt is from my soon to be published book entitled "I Will Come Myself." I am depending on the ladies of Magnificat to make this an overnight bestseller. Thanking you in advance.

Fr. Kevin, CM

The Sound of Music

I have always loved the sounds of the Advent Liturgy: the Rorate Coeli, the Mass of the Immaculate Conception, the majesty of the "O" Antiphons, the beautiful music of Christmas.

Since his election, Pope Benedict, himself a great lover of music, has drawn our attention to the need for a more devout Sacred Liturgy. It is not that we want to put the clock back and return to singing only Gregorian music; after all, there is quite a body of scripturally based music which is truly beautiful and anointed by the Holy Spirit. However, there is much that is not only very poor as a vehicle for divine worship, but is even theologically dubious. My local Catholic radio station broadcasts an inordinate amount of Christian rock music, even rap music, the lyrics of which are oftentimes indecipherable. I applaud their effort to reach out to the young, but nevertheless I have a real problem with this music. For one thing, I am not sure that rock, rap, hip-hop music can be baptized. At best it could be classed as entertainment, but I would question even that. Christian music should lead us into worship, but there is something about modern pop music which seems to preclude worship. However, this is just my opinion.

I heard someone recently give an example of the difference between entertainment music and worship music. He said, "You can sing the Tantum Ergo to the beautiful chant which was composed for it, or you can sing it to the tune of Old McDonald Had A Farm. The words remain the same, but whereas the first is undoubtedly a song of worship, the second is at best, a parody. A few years ago I resided at the funeral where, just before the burial rite at the Mass, as a tribute to the deceased man, they played Frank Sinatra singing "I Did It My Way." Unfortunately, the entertainment model has crept into the liturgy in many places. You have "Fr. Jay Leno" giving his monologue at the beginning of Mass. You may also have a music ministry which seems to be there to give a performance rather than to lead us in worship. On one occasion recently I asked whether we could have a period of silence after Holy Communion. I was told, "We don't do that here, Father." And they didn't.

I believe it is important for us to listen to the call of the Holy Father which is clearly the invitation of the Holy Spirit and begin a dialogue within our own communities about all of our liturgical music. Magnificat would be an ideal forum to debate this and influence what is happening at the local level.

May the cadences of Mary's song echo in your inner spirit and may the singing of the angels of Bethlehem fill your hearts during this time of Advent and Christmas. May you experience the presence of then Christ during the coming year.

Report of God's Death Greatly Exaggerated

Years ago at the university I came across "The Death of God" theology. I had just come home from Africa where they had never heard of it, but in the late sixties it was all the rage and I was reading Harvey Cox, et cetera, to keep up with the latest theological fad. Somehow or other I could not get excited about any of this. My simple Irish faith would not allow me to get my head around it. So I was consoled and amused to hear of Billie Graham's dialogue with the reporter who asked him if he had heard of "The Death of God" and did he believe it? The great man said, "No, I do not believe in it." The reporter then asked, "But how do you know it is not true? How do you know that God is not dead?" "I know," said Billy Graham, "because I spoke to Him this morning." End of conversation.

Today judging from what is happening in the world around us, you might be forgiven for thinking that God is indeed dead or at least that He has never revealed Himself. The ease with which modern men set aside God's revelation and arrogate the power that belongs only to God is astounding. And these are not people who have never heard of the commandments or the Gospels or the solemn teaching of the Church. People today are saying to God, "We know Your commandments, but we know better than You." Take an example like abortion, "thou shalt not kill". This is not hard to understand.

Pope Benedict XVI speaking recently in Rome said, "Secularization invades all aspects of daily life and causes the development of a mentality in which God is effectively absent, entirely or in part, from human life and conscience. This is not just an external threat to believers but has for some time been evident in the bosom of the Church herself. Hence people come to believe there is no longer any need for God, to think of him or return to him."

God in His mercy is patient with His children. But when we humans begin to put ourselves in place of Him and violate His commandments and usurp His work of giving and taking life, we tread on dangerous ground.

The followers of Christ need to be very clear when it comes to questions about what we believe and what we do. One of the most neglected of God's commandments is "honor your father and your mother" particularly the obligation of parents to form and train your children in the ways of God. Parents who neglect this task will be held accountable. God has revealed Himself to us. In every age of the Church he has raised up men and women to remind the faithful to adhere to His Word.

The Paschal Mystery is upon us and the victory of our Lord Jesus Christ is being celebrated once more. I pray for all my sisters in Magnificat to "make your home in God's Word" and open your heart to the voice of the Holy Spirit. Let Mary's words be always on your lips. "Be it done unto me according to Your Word." May the Risen Christ walk the road with you, may your hearts burn within you and may you also recognize Him in the breaking of the bread.

Truth and Consequences

Recently on a flight to Chicago I read two articles in the periodical "First Things." One was entitled "The Death of American Protestantism." This article dealt with the demise of the Protestant churches which formed the foundation of American religious belief and practice. America, it stated, is a Protestant country founded on the Biblical beliefs and principles of its early founders. It went on to describe the change that has taken place over time. It described the slow decline into secularism which has had the effect of reducing what were strong Biblical religious beliefs into nothing more than emotional uplift. This, as the writer pointed out, is especially true of the Episcopal church which has now reached the stage of accepting beliefs and practices that a few years ago would not even have been mentioned amongst seriously religious people.

The second article was quite different in that it was an account of the vindication of Pope Paul VI's now famous encyclical Humanae Vitae. The writer described what happened when this encyclical was published in 1968 and how it was ridiculed and made fun of by people outside of the Church and even by many inside. I can recall myself arriving at Catholic University just at the time of Humanae Vitae 's publication. I remember attending a gathering of heavy hitting theologians meeting solely for the purpose of denouncing Humanae Vitae and all it stood for.

The two articles were in marked contrast in that one described what happens when truth is wittingly or unwittingly eroded and the other, what happens when truth is held to and insisted upon. Pope Paul VI's letter has been vindicated, even by secular social scientists who now maintain that the introduction of artificial contraception was probably one of the worst things that has happened to modern society, and that even the worst fears of Pope Paul VI have been realized with all their disastrous consequences. We now have a situation where the population of some of the European countries is said to be in irreversible decline. Can you imagine a world without the Italians?

This is the world in which the Catholic Church is called upon to proclaim the truth. It is a world in which nearly everything is the subject of compromise and where the silence of Church ministers seems to approve of real moral indifference. An example is the silence of Church authorities concerning one of the worst forms of immorality namely the destruction of the child in its mother's womb. We Catholics simply cannot be silent on this matter whatever the consequence.

In an election year we of Magnificat must do all that we possibly can to promote an awareness of the, moral truths and values that are at stake in this election. We must pray earnestly that the truth of Christ and His Gospel be not compromised any more than they already have. The dictatorship of relativism has gone on for too long and has done much damage. We are never helpless in the face of situations like these because we can always pray. The power of our prayer to change events and even change the course of human history is well documented from the Battle of Lepanto to the fall of the Iron Curtain.

I wish you all a blessed vacation time and may I ask you to remember the poor who can never take a vacation.

Christic in His Word

S ometimes at Mass I have seen a deacon or a con-celebrating priest, after he has proclaimed the Gospel, hold the lectionary above his head and say, "And this, my brothers and sisters, is the Gospel of the Lord." I wouldn't mind if he said, "the Gospel of the Lord" and then held up the book. By what he does, he gives the impression that the book is the Gospel of the Lord. The book is simply a book which contains the written words of Sacred Scripture; when it is proclaimed and preached it is the living Gospel of Christ. A Bible can sit on a shelf for a hundred years; it becomes the Word of God when it is read out in the Church.

When, as a young priest, I read the Constitution on the Sacred Liturgy of the Second Vatican Council, I could not believe how profound and Spirit-filled it was and how it described the pre-eminence of Christ in the Liturgy of the Church. It made such sense to me. Perhaps the most outstanding passage is found in Chapter 1 Number 7, where the fathers of the Church describe the various ways in which Jesus is present in his people:

> Christ is always present in His Church, especially in her liturgical celebrations. He is present in the Sacrifice of the Mass not only in the person of his minister, "the same now offering, through the ministry of priests, who formerly offered himself on the cross," but especially in the Eucharistic species. By his power he is present in the sacraments so that when anybody baptizes it is really Christ himself who baptizes. He is present in his word since it is he himself who speaks when the holy scriptures are read in the Church. Lastly, he is present when the Church prays and sings, for he has promised "where two or three are gathered together in my name there am I in the midst of them (Mt. 18:20)."

Practicing Catholics have no problem believing that Jesus is present in the Eucharistic species under the appearance of bread and wine. We believe that it is no longer bread and wine, but the Body and Blood of Christ. It is this Presence of Christ that we receive in Holy Communion.

What many do not realize is that Jesus is just as present in His Word, since it is He Himself who speaks when the Sacred Scriptures are read in the Church. Jesus Himself is among us speaking to us as He did to His disciples. He begs us to attend to His voice and not to allow anything to distract us. That is why it is so necessary that readers should prepare well and pray themselves into the spirit and meaning of the sacred words. Above all, the priest should exercise great care about how he prepares his soul for the proclamation of the Holy Gospel. He should never lose the sense of Christ's presence to him as he reads and preaches, because he can never know how Jesus may speak to the hearts of his listeners. Once when I was a young priest, I preached what I thought was the worst homily I had ever prepared. As I walked from the Church after Mass, a young man came up to me with tears in his eyes and said, "Father, your beautiful homily moved me to tears. Would you please take a moment to hear my Confession?"

"Say but the word, and I shall be healed." Jesus Christ is present in His word. He points the way. He is the Truth. He gives us life.

St. John Vianney and the Year of the Priest

Pope Benedict XVI has announced a special Year of the Priesthood to begin on June 19 th, 2009, the Feast of the Sacred Heart and to end on the same date 2010. He did this to commemorate the 150th anniversary of the death of the great French priest St. John Vianney, Curé of Ars. During the course of this Year of the Priest, Pope Benedict will proclaim St. John Vianney as patron saint of all priests of the world. Up until now St, John Vianney has been patron saint of all parish priests.

St. John Vianney had many great struggles on his way to priestly ordination, not the least his difficulty with Latin and his seminary studies. Eventually he was ordained, but because his academic and other difficulties, his superiors assigned him to the Parish of Ars, an obscure country place where they were satisfied that if he didn't do much good, he probably wouldn't do much harm. There is a statue on the outskirts of the town of Ars depicting St. John Vianney speaking to a little boy. This commemorates an event that actually took place where St. John walking to Ars asked the boy to show him the way. The holy priest said to the boy, "if you show me the way to Ars, I will show you the way to heaven." That brief conversation is inscribed on the base of the statue.

There was a lot of opposition to this holy priests' ministry in Ars. Because of the love of Christ and the sweet fragrance of Christ which emanated from him, people were so won over and eventually he became one of the most famous priests in Europe. Even in his own lifetime, people were making pilgrimages to Ars so that they people could go to confession and receive his blessing. St. John Vianney captured the very essence of what it means to be a priest. Through his union with Jesus Christ which he cultivated through constant prayer and penance, his ministry made the reality of Christ's presence in the Eucharist and the Sacrament of Reconciliation palpable to all who experienced his priestly ministry. What St. Paul said of himself, St.

John Vianney could also say of himself: "my only desire is to proclaim Jesus Christ and Him crucified (I Cor. 1:20)."

The Curé of Ars once said, "The priest is the love of the heart of Christ." Pope Benedict has warned of the dilution of priestly ministry. He explained that without priests there would be no Eucharist and no mission.

We are all aware of the great crisis that has surrounded the priesthood for many years now, culminating in revelations and scandals which have taken a grave toll on the faith of many. This Year of the Priest is an opportunity for all, especially for we of Magnificat, to express our solidarity through prayer and pastoral love for those vessels of clay whom Christ has called to share in his priestly ministry. Many today are talking about the shortage of priests and suggesting how lay people might replace the ordained priest. This could never be a solution for the Church in any age because of the centrality of the priestly ministry to the sacramental and spiritual life of the Church. I hope that members of Magnificat, after prayer and invocation of the Holy Spirit, will be able to devise ways and means of supporting and helpful their Bishops and priests.

Fall 2009

This year 2009–2010 is the Year for Priests when the Church asks all the faithful to ponder on this unique gift of Christ to His Church. Priests are asked to look at the life and ministry of the patron of all priests, St. John M. Vianney, Curé of Ars. St. John Vianney would not have been voted by his class as the one most likely to succeed. His bishop, when he finally got around to ordaining him, sent him to Ars thinking perhaps that "if he does not do any good, he will probably not do much harm." On his way to Ars he met a boy and said to him, "If you show me the way to Ars, I will show you the way to heaven." He began his pastoral ministry there amongst a people who did not want him and did not want to hear his call to repentance. The rest is history. He never ceased to call them to conversion. He spent whole days and nights hearing their confessions and reconciling them to the Lord. He battled with Satan who threatened to destroy him and kill him. He never ceased to love all his flock, from the oldest to the youngest.

Like St. John Vianney, the priest is called to be another Christ and to act, as the Vatican Council reminds us, "in the person of Christ, the head of the Church." He belongs to Christ. One of my Vincentian confreres, who wrote a life of St. Vincent de Paul, described St. Vincent's famous moment of dedication to the service of the poor as his "conversion to the priesthood." This was indeed a moment of exceptional grace that changed Vincent from being just a good priest to becoming St. Vincent, the patron of all who serve the poor.

I pray that this grace be given to me and to every priest every day. If a priest wants to be loved by the people, he must be ready to be hated by them. If he wants to live a peaceful life he must be prepared to be persecuted. If he wants to experience richness in his life, he must be content to be poor.

The priest is not his own and he is never on his own. Jesus is with him always through the power and presence of His Holy Spirit.

"When the Spirit of truth comes, he will guide you into all the truth; for he will not speak on his own authority, but whatever he hears he will speak, and he will declare to you the things that are to come. He will glorify me, for he will take what is mine and declare it to you. All that the Father has is mine; therefore I said that he will take what is mine and declare it to you." (John 16:13-15)

I am well aware of the high esteem in which members of Magnificat hold the priesthood and you are aware of your associate priests value your contribution to the life of the Church. This Year for Priests will surely be a time for great grace not only for them, but for the whole Church. I ask you then to pray for priests and pray for particular priests of your own acquaintance that they may experience the transformed presence of Jesus in their lives and ministry.

Winter 2009

The Heat of the Day Indonesia Style

In October of 2009 the dynamic duo of Sr. Briege and myself set out for Indonesia to give two priests' retreats. We had been promised that the retreats would take place in a beautiful new hotel on the Island of Flores. Picture our surprise when we arrived to find the hotel only half finished and that instead of modern elevators, we had to endure the distinctly unmodern practice of climbing one hundred and two steps in tropical heat to the auditorium and chapel where the retreat was taking place. Air conditioning was nonexistent. The bright sunshine was plentiful, so a wonderful time was had by all. Yours truly grew in holiness by leaps and bounds during the two weeks. However, in spite of all of that, I must tell you that the retreats were wonderfully blessed by the Lord and grace flowed like a mighty river.

A feature of our visit to Indonesia were the days when we ministered to the laity in one of the flashiest hotels I have ever been in my life, the Mulia Hotel in Jakarta. We had two evenings for lay people which were attended on each occasion by seven thousand people. The tickets were issued from local parishes and were free; so lots of people, rich and poor, came. This was our third occasion to give such priest retreats in Indonesia. They were organized by a committee of lay people who have such great love for their priests and concern for their spiritual advancement, that they collected enough money to pay him for their travel to the retreat center and pay for their board and lodging during the retreat. In addition to that, they gave each priest a gift of a stole and a carrier bag. It is a real witness of lay participation in the local Church. Not only do they provide for such material needs, but they also befriend and pray for the priests who come.

One of the many wealthy families who is involved in this program owns a sugar plantation in another part of the country. They acquired it some years ago as a result of the original owner's financial difficulties. They even went to meet with Pope John Paul II to seek his advice about how they might best run this business. What they have done there is remarkable and an outstanding example of the Catholic Church's social teaching in practice. The plantation employs around fifty thousand people. This family decided from the beginning that they would provide good family accommodation for their workers, schools for their children, and free scholarships for every child who wanted it to attend elementary school, high school, and even college. I asked why they didn't use mechanized methods of harvesting the sugar cane. I was told that they decided from the beginning not to do this, because it would result in several thousands of their employees losing their jobs. This family business was established by a poor woman who escaped from China to Indonesia. She started a small family business which grew and expanded to the business empire that exists today. She was, by all accounts an exceptional woman, not only because of her social awareness, but also of her deep Catholic faith.

So the world is full of many surprises, and it is refreshing to meet people who take the Gospel and the teachings of the Church to heart. We are living now in times of Copernican change in the United States and in many parts of the world. The one thing however which can never change is the mystery of our faith in Jesus Christ. More than ever, it behooves us of Magnificat and the whole Church to proclaim the Lordship of Jesus Christ. May this time of Advent and the coming festival of the birth of Jesus be an occasion of great grace for all of us.

Wishing you every blessing in the heart of Jesus of Bethlehem,

Kevin Scallon, CM

Shamrocks and Shamrockery

When the Irish first landed on the shores of America, they were exceedingly poor. They lived poorly, they ate poorly and they worked hard. When it came to St. Patrick's Day, the only food they could afford to buy for a celebratory meal was corned beef and cabbage. Even in those days, corned beef and cabbage was the food of the poor, but no one could blame the poor Irish for thinking otherwise. To this day, corned beef and cabbage is the culinary choice of Irish Americans on St. Patrick's Day. Personally it would not be my first choice because of the impact it makes on the human digestive system. I know that it is sacrilegious to say this and I am sure that I will receive death threats from Irish men and women all over America, but I don't care. Someone has to be willing to be a martyr for the truth.

In addition to this exquisite cuisine, we have other customs which, to the FBI [foreign born Irish] seem strange indeed. The majestic rivers of America, magnificent to behold, are miraculously transformed on St. Patrick's Day to a green color which not even the bravest frog or the finest fish would dare to enter. To add insult to injury, if you go into a bar on St. Patrick's Day you would be served green beer. I have never drunk green beer, but I am sure it has a taste of the River Shannon to it. Then there are the many parades with their high-stepping drum majorettes. Whatever would the good Sisters have said?

St. Patrick himself was probably one of the greatest post-apostolic evangelizers in the history of the Church. He was kidnapped and came to Ireland as a slave while still in his teens. For several years he herded pigs on the hills of County Antrim, until finally he escaped and returned to his home in Southern Britain. In a dream he saw a young Irish man begging to return to Ireland. The young man in the dream said, "Oh holy youth, Patrick, come and walk among us once more." To make a long story short, Patrick went to France, received an education, was ordained a priest and then a bishop, and was sent back to Ireland where he began the work of evangelizing the Irish. He has written his autobiography called "The Confession of St. Patrick"* which every Catholic should read because it is such a beautiful and simple account of the life and apostolic labors of this great saint. He imparted a grace of faith to the Irish which has impelled them to go out to the whole world and bring the Gospel of Jesus Christ to every nation.

So the Irish Americans and all others who celebrate St. Patrick are doing a good thing. My banter about how they celebrate this feast is only in jest, though I still don't like corned beef and cabbage. Underlining all these customs there is a foundation of gold on which these poor Irish built a magnificent Church, here in the land of the free in the home of the brave. We Irish look on Patrick as the Jews look on Abraham. He is our father in the faith. He is our friend and has been our patron and protector through good times and bad, and God knows there have been plenty of both, especially the bad. So pay no attention to the ranting of an aging FBI person. When St. Patrick's day comes, raise a glass of emerald green beer, and toast St. Patrick as you sit down to your corned beef and cabbage.

* The text of The Confession of St. Patrick [cf. http://www.ccel.org/ccel/patrick/confession.toc.html]

Summer 2010

Bread, Butter, Jam and faith

Mrs. O'Sullivan-Clarke, the wife of the station-master in my home town in Ireland, was from Skibbereen in County Cork. How she got to Irvinestown, I'm not really sure, but it was probably because her husband worked in Cork, and got a job as station-master up north. It was long ago, before Ireland was partitioned. I arrived under her care on a September morning when I was five years old. Mrs. Clarke was a formidable looking woman, with what I thought then was a very leathery looking face; but since than I have revised my opinion, considering the condition of my own skin at the moment. It took me quite a while to understand her Cork accent, but I eventually mastered it. When she said things like, 'If you don't behave, I'll put a pin in your back," I realized she wasn't talking about a pin, but a pain.

When I first met her, Mrs. Clarke had been a widow for several years. She was my teacher, but had no real qualifications. The parish priest had employed her to teach what passed then for kindergarten simply because she was a smart woman in need of employment. One of the many things she did for us was to make us aware of the importance of our Catholic faith. She was clearly a good, religious person with a strong living faith. In those days, the children at our little primary school came from quite poor homes, Mrs. Clarke arranged for the parish priest to come in once a week to visit us. She trained us to stand up and say "Good morning, Father," and the priest would reply, "Good morning, children." Then out of a paper bag, he would produce a large loaf of bread, a pound of butter and a pot of homemade jam. He would speak to us for a few minutes, replace his hat, then he would leave. We all said in unison, "God bless you, Father and thank you very much." Immediately after his departure, the loaf was sliced, buttered, spread with jam and enjoyed by all of us. We enjoyed the weekly celebration.

The other thing Mrs. Clarke did was to encourage us to support the foreign missions in this unusual form. There was a community of sisters in Ireland called the Sisters of the Holy Rosary who worked in Nigeria and several other African Countries. Each year they would send posters around to all the schools with a big rosary printed on them and photographs of little African children. Mrs. Clarke would encourage us all to bring pennies for, as she put it, "the black babies in Africa." We gave Mrs. Clarke a penny and she perforated one of the beads on the poster, and assured us that our contribution would bring about the salvation of one of these black babies. She had many ways of making us aware of our duties as baptized Catholics, and while you might say she was poor at handing on academic knowledge, she was very rich in handing on the faith and a love for Christ and the Church. Just the fact that I am writing about her at this moment, is an indication of how powerful an impression was made on me.

After I was ordained, I returned to my native town to say Mass. By this time Mrs. Clarke was long retired and living quietly in her own home. She attended the Mass and the celebratory meal afterwards, and she treated me as if I were the Pope himself.

The Holy Spirit blows where He wills, and I have learned over the years, that He teaches the most profound lessons to the most insignificant people. As parents and members of the Church, we should never underestimate the impression we make on others by what we say and do. I have often remarked that the greatest lesson I received about the importance of prayer was from looking at my father and mother leading us in the family rosary in our own kitchen. Today there are very powerful formative forces acting on the minds and spirits of our young people. But in spite of everything, we must never forget that the most powerful influence at work in all of us is the grace of the Holy Spirit. We have just celebrated the great feast of Pentecost where the Holy Father reminded us that without Pentecost there would be no Church, and without Mary, there would be no Pentecost. This poor girl could never in her wildest dreams have imagined how the Lord would use her. When Jesus began the work of founding His Church, He chose twelve men, to be with Him, to proclaim the Good News, and to overcome the powers of darkness in the world.

Look at Magnificat and how beautifully it has flourished in the Church. This is happening because a few of you in the beginning listened to the Spirit and followed His inspiration. The evidence is there for all of us to see. We have seen it, we have experienced it, we have lived it, and this beautiful Magnificat Ministry has enriched our personal lives, our family lives, and our Church.

Nora O'Sullivan-Clarke may never be canonized by the Church, but I have canonized her, and I am sure that she would be delighted at the thought!

October 2010

"THE PAX "

A little understood gesture in the liturgy is the offering of the sign of peace. You can hardly find anyone who really understands its true significance. In many places, it is simply ignored by the priest, in others, it is the mandatory Sunday morning parish hug accompanied by kindly remarks and little jokes. It is a nice moment of little or no significance.

And yet, the sign of peace or "the pax", as some of us older people might know it, is a very important liturgical gesture as old as the gospel itself. "Therefore, if you are offering your gift at the altar and there remember that your brother has something against you, leave your gift there in front of the altar. First go and be reconciled to your brother; then come and offer your gift." [Matthew 5:23-24]

Taught by the Holy Spirit, the Church has included this important instruction of Christ in the liturgy at the moment when we are preparing to receive Christ himself in the Eucharist. She does this to remind us of these words of the Lord, so that we may offer the gift [of ourselves] to the Father, only after we have first been reconciled with all our brothers and sisters.

The sign of peace, far from being an empty gesture, is in fact a solemn matter which we should take to heart. So if Aunt Mary Jane hasn't spoken to her daughter since she got married in the registry office twenty years ago, she really has to do something about it. Similarly, with Patrick Goodcatholic who refuses to forgive his neighbor over some never-to-be forgotten incident that could have been settled long ago over a beer. The "pax" then is a gesture of peace, and if it is not a true gesture, we really ought to think hard about it, maybe as preparation for a good searching general confession.

What we have now, and who's to blame for it, is a kind of compressed liturgical happy hour where people hug each other and have mini conversations and say "love you." In Ireland we may even talk about the weather. And at the risk of sounding like Andy Rooney, I am not ready for "rib cracking bear hugs" [manly of course] from some total stranger just before receiving the Eucharist. It really can be a huge distraction at what should be a sacred moment before Holy Communion. I have no solution to this dilemma, but I am sure someone has one. Meanwhile, we of Magnificat, should begin a quiet campaign to restore reverence to this beautiful gesture, and make it what the Holy Spirit intended it to be, a welcoming of Christ into our midst.

December 2010

In this issue, we wanted to use a few of Fr. Kevin's own words to priests and laity alike from his book, I Will Come Myself. Jesus always ministers to us through His priests.

"I will finish this work with the beautiful words of Pope Benedict XVI which he addresses to Mary, Star of the Hope: Through you, through your 'yes', the hope of the ages became reality, entering this world and its history. You bowed low before the greatness of this task and gave your consent: 'Behold, I am the handmaid of the Lord; let it be to me according to your word' (Luke 1:38). When you hastened with holy joy across the mountains of Judea to see your cousin Elizabeth, you became the image of the Church to come, which carries the hope of the world in her womb across the mountains of history. But alongside the joy which, with your Magnificat, you proclaimed in word and song for all the centuries to hear, you also knew the dark sayings of the prophets of the suffering of the servant of God in this world … you saw the growing power of hostility and rejection which built up around Jesus until the hour of the Cross, when you had to look upon the Savior of the world, the heir of David, the Son of God dying like a failure, exposed to mockery, between criminals. Then you received the word of Jesus: 'Woman, behold your Son!' (John 19:26). From the cross you became a mother in a new way: the mother of all those who believe in your Son Jesus and wish to follow him. (Spe Salvi: 50)

Mary is the promised woman of the Old Testament. She enters the history of salvation as the one chosen by God to be the mother of our Savior Jesus Christ. Through her, Jesus speaks to a world waiting to be delivered from sin: 'I will come Myself (and cure him)'

(Matthew 8:7). Mary draws us closer to her Son. The last words she speaks in the Gospels are, in effect, her final words: 'Do whatever He tells you' (John 2:5). And so, Mary not only brought Christ to the world of the past, she teaches us the way we must go in the present if we are to experience the power of the Risen Christ."

February 2011

"I have called you and you are mine"
Isaiah 43:1

It may take a village to raise a child, but it takes a family to produce a vocation. Lately I have thought about the meaning of vocation and how God calls certain people.

Not long ago, I met a young man in the last year of his seminary training. He was a deacon. He told me how different it had been for him to answer his vocation. He talked about the reaction his parents when he announced to them that he wanted to become a priest. They were less than enthusiastic. In fact, they expressed their extreme disappointment and disapproval of the whole idea. Both his parents were what you might call "a la carte" Catholics who possessed more than their share of the false enlightenment of our time. They remained resolutely opposed to every step of his journey through the seminary towards the priesthood.

Holy orders in my own time, parents welcomed the news that their son or daughter had decided to follow their vocation. Brothers and sisters were equally delighted that such a grace had been bestowed on their family; that God had chosen one of their own. They supported the chosen one in every possible way. My own brothers and sisters supported me by the power of their example, the integrity of their lives and their active faithful sacramental life. Sure, they had wives and families to provide for. They had jobs to go to and businesses to run. But I could see that their Catholic faith came before all else, even into old age they continue to live like this and they have handed on the same faith to their sons and daughters.

For better or for worse, we get all our values from our parents. When a parent tells a child how to live by God's truth there is a powerful anointing of the Holy Spirit on that word and they never forget it as long as they live. No one ever had to tell me of the importance of confession. I saw my father go when I was a boy.

I don't think we quite realize the depth of the darkness that has enveloped our world where grossest forms of immoral behavior are taken to be normal. We of Magnificat have a heavy duty to live our vocation in Christ Jesus and to shed the light of Christ wherever we are. Jesus said, "I am the light of the world (John 8:12)." It is the essence of every vocation to let this light shine and to dispel the darkness. Jesus also said, "I have overcome the world. (John16:33)" He has promised to be with the Church and that the gates of hell will never win the victory. The mystery of vocation confronts us all at some point in our life, and the newest doctor of the Church has given to us the most marvelous teaching which she called her "Little Way;" namely that "serving God is not done in mighty deeds, but with the love of a humble and obedient heart."

The theme of our conference to be held in March is "In Christ, a New Creation." This new creation is brought about through our Baptism into Christ Jesus. Christ who in his own baptism sanctified the waters of our baptism. Our baptism into Christ is the pearl of great price. It is the very essence of our vocation. Let us pray that all who attend, and all who participate in this upcoming conference, may receive a great anointing of the Holy Spirit. May Mary, the Immaculate Mother of Jesus, the spouse of the Holy Spirit, pray for us. Amen.

Chapter 16 Flame of Divine Love

The foundation of the edifice of the Church is the Sacraments of Initiation-Baptism, Confirmation and Eucharist. Christ comes to live within us; it is no longer we who live, but Christ who lives in us (Cf. Galatians 2:20) The life of Baptism is made strong by Confirmation and the manifold gifts of the Holy Spirit. It is nourished by Jesus, the Bread of Life, in the Holy Eucharist.

Through the action of the Holy Spirit, we understand what Baptism does to the soul- that through it we are born into new life in Christ, that Original Sin is forgiven along with all other sins, that we become children of the Father, that we recognize Jesus as our Savior and our brother, and that we are made holy by the presence of love of the Holy Spirit. We literally become temples of the Holy Trinity. What a pity that so many people do not have a clearer understanding of what Baptism does. It does make us children of God; it transforms our soul and marks it with a character, an irreversible uniqueness which lasts into eternity. Once baptized, always baptized.

I often wonder as I baptize their children if parents realize the seriousness of the duty they undertake. Do they realize that the God who gives them children will also hold them responsible for how they have instructed their children and taught them to follow Christ and to walk in the ways of righteousness? God's plan is that every child will become a saint. Parents must help their children to hear God's word and to live out their Baptismal promises to reject Satan and his ways, and to always be open to the Spirit who comes in power at Confirmation. Parental witness is the best teacher of all.

Today parents have to keep guard over their children and not abandon them to be formed by the influences of the secular world. Parents have a moral duty to teach their children, protect their innocence, and instruct them in Christian moral values. In earlier times, young people absorbed such values from the communities in which they grew up. Sadly this is no longer the case.

Why is Baptism so important? It is important because it is the foundation stone of Christian life. It is the most important of all the sacraments, because it gives us a share in the life and mysteries of Jesus Christ. Baptized people no longer belong to themselves, but to God. Like Jesus, they are called to be servants, to profess their faith openly, to be part of the Church's mission, to establish God's Kingdom on earth. At Baptism they begin a life of discipleship, following and obeying the Gospel of Jesus Christ proclaimed by the Church, even to the shedding of their blood.

August 2011

Dear Magnificat Central Service Team,
Fr. Kevin anniversary collage
Fr. Kevin celebrating Mass during his 50th Anniversary

There are moments in everyone's life when the Lord gives us opportunities to give thanks. My recent Golden Jubilee was one such moment. I thank the Lord particularly for allowing me to serve Him in priestly ministry for such a long time. Over the years I have been blessed with many great friends all of whom have enriched my life and have been a great support to me in my priestly service.

I would like to take this opportunity to thank you for your prayers, your support and your generosity at this special moment in my life. I will be offering a Triduum of Masses for your intentions.

With every best wish,
Yours Sincerely in Jesus Christ,
Fr. Kevin Scallon, CM

"Mary draws us closer to her Son. The last words she speaks in the Gospels are, in effect, her final words: 'Do whatever He tells you' (John 2:5). And so, Mary not only brought Christ to the world of the past, she teaches us the way we must go in the present if we are to experience the power of the Risen Christ."

October 2011

I hope you had a good summer, at least better than my own. At one point, I had cellulitis in my left leg and phlebitis in my right leg and a kidney infection. I was limping like a wounded hero and working my fingers to the bone. Apart from that, I was grand. Summer for myself and Sr. Briege means almost continuous work with the "Intercession for Priests" in England and in Ireland for the entire month of August. At the end of it all I was exhausted, but I hasten to reassure you that I am fine now. My left leg is perfect, my right leg is, if possible, even better and the rest of me is grand. It is amazing what a few days of sunshine and the waters of the Gulf of Mexico can do for the battered human condition.

My good friend Shane O'Dougherty spent fourteen and a half years in Wormwood Scrubs (what a name for a prison), London, for being a member of the Irish Republican Army and doing desperate things for the "cause of Irish freedom." While in prison, Shane encountered Christ in the pages of the Gospel and by reading the life of St. Padre Pio. His conversion experience was nothing short of Pauline. He is a monument to the grace of Christ, and all these years later, remains an outstanding Catholic layman who repudiates every form of violence and whose love for the Church and our Blessed Lady is unique.

Shane has been trying for years to get me to go with him on his annual visit to Lourdes , Our Lady of Lourdes, and Garabandal, of which he is a great devotee. Finally, after having said, "Yes," we set out and flew to Bilbao where we rented a car and drove to Lourdes. Shane is a man of great directness and tremendous humor. He said, "This is what we are going to do. We are going to stay in Lourdes tonight. We will get up early in the morning and go down to have a bath as Our Lady has directed all pilgrims." He knocked on my door next morning, handed me a cup of coffee and said, "Get dressed." I had often been to Lourdes, but only once ever went to the baths. He persuaded me that this is one of the things that our Blessed Mother asks of all the pilgrims who go to Lourdes. I reminded him that my memory was that priests got preferential option, meaning they were allowed to go first. What happens is you go into a cubicle that holds about a dozen people. You strip down to your jockey shorts, which I did, sitting and thinking of nothing in particular. Sitting around were German theologians, English canons, Filipino bishops and your faithful servant. We were not a pretty sight and I almost laughed out loud at the thought at how the Lord reduces our importance to jockey shorts. After that, I went into the place of the baths and I was assisted by holy men from somewhere in the world who helped me down into the pool of frigid sanctifying water, and then helped to dunk me into this. Shane later said that the gasp that came from me at that moment was heard as far away as Paris, maybe even Dublin.

Humor aside, the experience was truly mystical, and Our Lady's promise to bring healing to my sickly frame was answered completely. She fixed me good. Afterwards I met up with Shane who said, "Now we have to go to Confession." So we went to the confessional chapel near the shrine and I found myself sitting in front of a Holy Ghost Father from Ireland who spent his life in Sao Paulo, Brazil. We chatted for quite a long time and then I began to wonder if he would ever hear my Confession. After that we went to breakfast in a place of Shane's choosing and in due course said "Adieu" to Lourdes and were on our way to Garabandal.

Yours Sincerely in Jesus Christ,
Fr. Kevin

December 2011

"… And this will be a sign for you: you will find an infant wrapped in swaddling clothes and lying in a manager." (Luke 2:12)

He had been on the road for a little over an hour when something started to happen to his little Mazda car. The lights kept getting dimmer and dimmer. Suddenly they went out and the car stopped. All attempts to start it again failed. He still had a long drive ahead of him. It was the evening of Christmas day and he had not seen a car or a human being since he left Dublin. His old aunt had died the day before and was to be buried the next day. Her nephew, the priest, would celebrate her funeral Mass.

He was stranded on the side of the road at nine o'clock on Christmas night. By the light of the Christmas moon he saw a cottage on the far side of the road directly across from where he was parked. There was a light burning in the window. This was long before the age of the cell phone, so he decided to ask the people in the house for the use of their phone. He went through a little white wooden gate, up the path, and knocked on the door. After a moment, a young man with a beard opened the door. Looking past him into the house, the priest saw a young woman with a baby in her arms. She was holding the baby close to her cheek. She smiled at the priest who was telling the man what had happened. He asked if they had a phone. The man replied very gently, "No we don't have a phone, but if you walk back to the town there is a man with a bicycle shop. He will let you use his phone. You can't miss the house it is next to the supermarket. He will not mind if you wait there until someone comes to pick you up." The priest thanked the couple and wished them a Happy Christmas. "Will the car be alright there he asked the man?" "Oh yes, I'll see to that", he replied. On that bright moonlit night the priest walked back to town to look for the bicycle shop. He was distracted by his encounter with the couple and their baby, and by the strange aroma in the house. It was not an Irish smell. For some reason it reminded him of his recent visit to the Holy Land and why was the house only lit by candles?

The owner of the bicycle shop opened the door, and the priest told him about his predicament and what happened to his car. "Would you mind if I used your phone to call my nephew to come and pick me up?" he asked. The nephew promised he would be there within the hour. The bicycle-man's wife offered him tea and Christmas cake which he gladly accepted. She talked about the weather and how Christmas was so quiet this year, and how the price of everything seemed to be increasing all the time. She told him how their daughter phoned them from Australia, and how she had spent part of Christmas day at the beach. There were many families around here that had someone out foreign (overseas). "Sure Father, you must be exhausted after all your preparations 'for the Christmas'." The priest sighed in agreement. The woman talked while her husband peacefully smoked his pipe enjoying the warmth of the turf fire on his feet.

The nephew arrived within the hour. They said goodbye to the bicycle-man and his wife, and wished them a Happy Christmas once more. They stopped at the priest's stricken vehicle to discover that the fan belt was missing. They would return to take the car the next day.

When the funeral was over, they went with a local mechanic to fetch the car. Having had the repair work done, the priest turned to pay a visit to the young family across the road. As he headed for the little white gate, he could not find it. There was only the hedge row, and beyond it an open field. There was no house in sight.

On the return journey the nephew spoke incessantly. The priest never uttered a word. It was the Feast of the Holy Family.

Yours Sincerely in Jesus Christ,
Fr. Kevin

March 2012

Pope Benedict XVI in his "Motu Proprio: Porta Fidei" has declared the Year of Faith beginning October 11, 2012. In it he describes what his vision is for this Year of Faith. He has in mind a time to pay special attention to the meaning of faith. Every Sunday we proclaim the Creed which contains the foundational truth of the faith of Christians: belief in God the Father and all that he has revealed to us in Jesus Christ and in the Holy Spirit; concluding with belief in the Holy Catholic Church and all that Jesus has given to us through the Church.

I need hardly tell you how much our faith is being challenged and even denied in this present age. Even in the developed nations, men and women, communities and governments are acting as if God did not exist and as though He had never revealed Himself to mankind. We construe for ourselves systems of belief and behavior which satisfy our own desires. We have only to consider modern attitudes toward sanctity of human life and human sexuality to realize how far removed we have become from faith in what God has revealed to us. All of this and many other issues are undoubtedly having the effect of eroding divine faith, even in people of the Church. We wonder why young people are losing their faith so rapidly and so completely, but no one dares to question their lifestyle and in particular, their attitude toward their own sexuality and the sexuality of others, and the devastating effects of pornography which has become so acceptable. Everybody knows and many acknowledge what is going on, but there are few willing to speak out for fear of being politically incorrect. Enter Pope Benedict to remind us that we are the salt of the earth and light of Christ in this world.

We cannot accept that salt should become tasteless or the light be kept hidden (cf. Mt 5:13–16). The people of today can still experience the need to go to the well, like the Samaritan woman, in order to hear Jesus, who invites us to believe in Him and to draw upon the source of living water welling up within Him (cf. Jn 4:14). We must rediscover a taste for feeding ourselves on the word of God, faithfully handed down by the Church, and on the bread of life, offered as sustenance for His disciples (cf. Jn 6:51). Indeed, the teaching of Jesus still resounds in our day with the same power: "Do not labor for the food which perishes, but for the food which endures to eternal life" (Jn 6:27). The question posed by His listeners is the same that we ask today: "What must we do, to be doing the works of God?" (Jn 6:28). We know Jesus' reply: "This is the work of God, that you believe in Him whom He has sent" (Jn 6:29). Belief in Jesus Christ, then, is the way to arrive definitively at salvation. (Porta Fidei: para.3)

The Holy Father in everything he writes is emphatic about the uniqueness of Jesus as the Son of God and Saviour of mankind. Even this central doctrine of our faith is questioned by many who should know better. We have all heard people saying things like "Buddha, Jesus, and Mohammed; they are all the same. What's the difference? They are all leading in the same direction." There is an enormous difference. Jesus is the only begotten Son of God the Father. He took our humanity in the womb of the Virgin Mary. He died on the cross to save us from sin and death. This is the faith of the Church and it is our faith. And the Church must always be true to the task that Jesus has imposed upon Her; namely to go out to all nations and proclaim the truth of the Gospel to people everywhere baptizing them in the name of the Father, the Son and the Holy Spirit.

Faith is a divine virtue which we receive when we are baptized, but which can lie dormant in a soul, sometimes for an entire lifetime. This divine gift has to be nourished by contemplating God's Word, by heeding the call to repentance, by being nourished at the Table of the Eucharist, and by being enlightened and strengthened by the grace of the Holy Spirit.

Without these sources of divine grace, God can recede into a distant place within our lives and be forgotten. Pope Benedict has often expressed this fear. St. Paul tells us that faith comes through hearing. The Holy Father is asking us to listen again to the truth of Christ proclaimed every day in the Church, and particularly at the Sunday Eucharist; to listen in prayer to the inspiration that comes to us each day from the Holy Spirit.

We must also approach Mary, the Mother of the Church and

first disciple of Jesus. She can teach us how to respond in faith and how to witness to this faith everyday.

Yours Sincerely in Jesus Christ,
Fr. Kevin

"Faith is a divine virtue which we receive when we are baptized, but which can lie dormant in a soul, sometimes for an entire lifetime. This divine gift has to be nourished by contemplating God's Word, by heeding the call to repentance, by being nourished at the Table of the Eucharist, and by being enlightened and strengthened by the grace of the Holy Spirit."

July 2012

"For Good Men to Do Nothing?"

Returning from Ireland recently, I felt downcast over the state of affairs there. So much has gone wrong in the Church: so many disappointments, so many failures, and worse then anything, such virulent criticism and opposition to the Bishops and clergy. This is not something we have experienced in Ireland until recently. While in Europe, Sr. Briege and I went to England to give a parish retreat. On this retreat we met some English Catholics who were not the kind of people I would normally associate with. They were the from the upper echelons of English society; a party of about twenty people with Sr. Briege, myself and the parish priest. I was quite astonished at how proud they were of their Catholic faith, how utterly respectful they were of the Church, and how lovingly they cherished their good priest who had served them over the years.

Then I returned to the U.S. One of the first things I experienced was the interview on EWTN with Raymond Arroyo, Cardinal Wuerl and Archbishop Lori. As you may know, it concerned pending legislation affecting religious freedoms here in the United States. This was a wake-up call to me because of the seriousness with which these two churchmen viewed the outcome of the establishment of such legislation in the country. What concerned me was that they saw it as a very real threat to the freedom to practice religion here in the U.S. They were asked about the unity of the hierarchy on this matter and they assured us that the Bishops were united to a man and determined that they would not yield in the matter. They also referred to the government's steely determination to not even discuss any further what was intended in the new law. It was as though both sides had drawn a line in the sand and were saying "thus far and no further."

What disturbed me also is how closely it reflected what appears to be happening in my own little country. For quite a while now the government and the public media have been conducting a campaign of defamation and vilification of the Catholic clergy and certain Catholic Bishops in particular. They are also threatening to take over the Catholic school system and strip it of any reference to Catholicism or Christian faith. They are not even subtle anymore about their intentions. One hesitates to be conspiratorial about governments and movements in culture and society, but it is becoming very clear to me that there are forces at work here in the United States and certainly in Europe that are no longer willing to tolerate influences or authority that are not coming directly from the state. It seems that there is to be no room for religion and religious experience in the public square.

The framers of the American Constitution were very careful to include freedom of conscience and freedom of religion because they were aware of the important part that religion plays in the life of the individual and in the life of society in general. These were not foolish or stupid men. Edmund Burke, the Anglo-Irish Parliamentarian, famously warned that "for evil to triumph it is sufficient for good men to do nothing."

The Holy Spirit is guiding counsels of Cardinal Dolan and his fellow Bishops. I am so proud of Cardinal Dolan's interventions and of the Bishops on EWTN. The final stroke which convinced me of the seriousness of their intent was when Archbishop Lori stressed their call for a "Fortnight for Freedom." I was overjoyed when I heard the importance which he laid on these two weeks of intercessory prayer. However, my joy in this was tinged with sadness when I realize that my own Irish Bishops, in all the years of the troubles and in the present crisis in the Catholic Church in Ireland, never even once asked the people to pray. Had they done so, I am sure that the Lord would have heeded His people and healed them long, long before now.

Prayer is the heart of Magnificat. Here is something that the Lord has put before us. During these two weeks, June 21st (the vigil of the Feasts of St. John Fisher and St. Thomas More) to July 4th (Independence Day), we must pray concerning all of these issues. We must go before the Lord and plead that He will help us, and deliver us from this darkness. We must take up our Rosary in this Lepanto-like crusade both in Europe and in the United States. We must beg Our Lady of Victory to help the Church now as she did then. May the Holy Spirit pour out upon you the grace of zeal for the House of God at this moment. And may I wish you every blessing and a great outpouring of the gifts of the Spirit into your lives and communities.

Yours Sincerely in Jesus Christ,
Fr. Kevin

October 2012

Prophecies from Lourdes

I am sure you are all reading the book "Harbinger" by Jonathan Cahn, and even though it is a novel, for me it has proved to be an extraordinary read. While going through it I was reminded of a document I received some years ago concerning prophecies of Our Lady to St. Bernadette of Lourdes which she was told to pass on to Pope Leo XIII (which is another story). There were five prophecies in all.

St. Bernadette

The first one dealing with the fact that Lourdes would become a famous center of healing after the death of St. Bernadette. This, of course, is what has happened. The second concerned the invention of electricity. The third foretold the second World War and the devastation of Europe. The fourth predicted man would walk on the moon, before the Wright brothers were even born. As you know, all of these prophecies have been fulfilled and have come to pass, some even in our own time.

Now let me quote to you the words of the fifth and final prophecy:

"Your Holiness, the Virgin has told me that when the 20th century passes away, with it will pass away the Age of Science. A new Age of Faith will dawn around the world. Proof will come at last that it was Our Lord Who created the world and man, and this will be the beginning of the end for the scientists, in whom the people will cease to believe. Millions will return to Christ, and as the numbers of believers swell, the power of the Church will grow as never before. Also causing many to turn their backs on science will be the arrogance of physicians who use their knowledge to create an abomination. These doctors will find the means to combine the essence of a man and the essence of a beast.

The people will know in their hearts that this is wrong, but they will be powerless to stop the spawning of such monsters. In the end they will hunt scientists down as ravening wolves are hunted. On the eve of the year 2000, a final clash between the followers of Mohammed and the Christian nations of the world will take place. A furious battle will be waged in which 5,650,451 soldiers are killed and a bomb of great power will fall on a city in Persia. But in the fullness of time the sign of the cross will prevail and all of Islam will be forced to convert to Christianity. There will follow a century of peace and joy as all the nations of the earth lay down their swords and shields. Great prosperity will follow as the Lord showers His blessings down upon the faithful. No family on earth will know poverty or hunger. One person in ten will be granted by God the power to heal and they will cast out all sicknesses from those who seek their aid. Many will rejoice at these miracles. The 21st Century will come to be known as the Second Golden Age of Mankind."

The prophecy declares that "a new Age of Faith will dawn around the world." Perhaps it is no coincidence that we are being reminded of these words of the Blessed Mother of God in a year set aside by the present Holy Father as a "Year of Faith." Pope John Paul II spoke frequently about the new springtime that was coming for the Church and for the world. We in Magnificat know that the problems of the present time are not amenable to human solutions, but can only be resolved with the sovereign power of our merciful Savior. Our Lady's words to St. Bernadette are words of great hope, of an outpouring of Divine Grace that will transform the Church and all the world. Let us pray that God's perfect will and plan for His Church and for our little planet will come to pass in every detail, so that the 21st century will indeed become the "Second Golden Age of Mankind."

P.S. Regarding the upcoming Presidential election, I find the actions of the present administration regarding the HHS mandate, infringing on the religious rights and freedoms of Catholics and contrary to our Church teachings, very disturbing indeed. I pray that the American people will choose wisely.

December 2012

In the Crossing of My Arms

Ever since I read the first book about Guadalupe I developed a great desire to go there on pilgrimage. Thanks to Marilyn Quirk and Magnificat, I fulfilled this spiritual desire in November 2012.

The tradition of going on pilgrimage is as old as the Church. Pilgrimage is a journey inspired by the Holy Spirit to seek some significant grace for one's life. In the early Church, Jerusalem was the place, then Rome and other places. And recently Guadalupe, Lourdes, Fatima, Knock and Medjugorje are sites of pilgrimage. The El Camino is the famous route stretching across Northern Spain that is still traversed by thousands to the Shrine of St. James of Compostela, recently highlighted by the movie "The Way."

For me, the pilgrimage was special for the many interior graces that came to me. I was led to pray and intercede for many people and intentions with great awareness and fervor.

I was deeply impressed by the devotion of the local people for whom the faith was obviously such an integral part of their lives. Their Catholicism was normal for them. Jesus is their friend and Our Lady of Guadalupe one of the family. There was no shame or embarrassment in them. We encountered a small group at the Church of the apparitions who had walked for five days to come to the Shrine. Some of the young men told us that they were discerning about becoming priests. Their faith and devotion brought tears to our eyes. That was the kind of spiritual air we breathed all the time. It seemed prayer was easy for everyone.

The old original Basilica was charming, but too small; the new one much more functional, accommodating several thousand pilgrims. Like the Basilica at Knock, this large building could do with a few artistic geniuses to bring it to life with great art.

The Tilma too seemed remote and definitely needs to be

97

repositioned and brought closer so that the people can gaze on it and venerate it. Modern technology should surely be able to bring this about without compromising safety or due reverence. But that is just my opinion.

There are two great images in the world that stand out above all others. One is the Shroud of Turin, the other the Tilma of Our Lady of Guadalupe. Mary is the Mother of Life in a world benighted by the culture of death. She is and always will be a relevant presence to humankind. I am glad to have been in her living presence and to have come under her loving gaze. I pray that this first Magnificat pilgrimage may bring many graces to Magnificat throughout the world. Her words to St. Juan Diego never fail to move me:

"Am I not here, I, who am your Mother? Are you not under my shadow and protection? Am I not the source of your joy? Are you not in the hollow of my mantle, in the crossing of my arms?"

The Tears of Rachel

When the tragedy of Sandy Hook Elementary happened, everyone was shocked to the core of their being. Immediately all the talk was of guns and what to do about them. All very natural, given the number of families involved. I listened to the endless reporting, talk and analysis. However, the one word that was consistently missing from it all was the word evil. This was a profoundly evil act committed by a young man who was clearly under the influence of a force that impelled him to act in this way. The word sin did not get a mention in the tsunami of words and talk even though a powerful force of sin was at work. What is it about us that we seem unable to face this terrible truth, and that ours is a very sinful society?

We are being asked to "repent of our guns," but not of our sin. People blame God for allowing such tragedies to take place, but no one is blaming the forces of darkness whose evil hand is at work here. There should be a movement of repentance and reparation to God for this savage attack on His sacred gift of life. We need to repent of our sins and ask the Father to heal our society in the name of his Son who cried out, "I have come so that you may have life" (John 10:10). "The Lord weeps" for His little ones and for the frustration of His beautiful plan that He had for their lives stretching into the years and decades ahead. He weeps for the generations that will now never be because this evil has come to pass.

Right now in Ireland, there is a great struggle taking place between our government and the Church over proposed legislation to make abortion legal. Pray that God may sovereignly intervene to prevent this from happening. The other day a sobering thought came to my mind, that since Roe vs. Wade, the number of abortions which have taken place in the U.S. is more than five times the entire population of the island of Ireland. This is a sin of unimaginable gravity. Much prayer and fasting is needed now more than ever.

"Then was fulfilled what was spoken by the prophet Jeremiah: 'A voice was heard in Ramah, wailing and loud lamentation, Rachel weeping for her children; she refused to be consoled, because they were no more'." (Matthew 2:17-18).

May the Lord continue to inspire you in your many apostolates and may He bless your loved ones by a great outpouring of the grace of His Holy Spirit.

May 2013

Strong in Faith (1 Peter 5:9)

At the heart of the New Evangelization is the proclamation and experience of the person of Jesus. The reason for the uniqueness of Magnificat and other such movements is that we have had exactly such an experience of Christ through Baptism in the Holy Spirit. Others are not so fortunate because, for one reason or another, they have not been exposed to this type of proclamation. Even many clergy who have not experienced Christ in this way find it difficult to feel the anointing of the Holy Spirit, who alone can cause us to encounter the living risen Christ.

The Holy Spirit will always bear witness to the truth of Christ when it is proclaimed. He will penetrate the minds and hearts of those who listen to and assent to such truth. We have all experienced this and seen it for ourselves. The word of the Lord proclaimed is the word of Jesus; it is Jesus the Word.

The first way we proclaim Christ is by our Baptism. Through Baptism, we live in Jesus Christ and He lives in us. We are the "sweet fragrance of Christ" (2 Cor. 2:15) before we utter a word or offer a helping hand. This proclamation of Christ is greatly enhanced through our sacramental life of Baptism, Confirmation, Eucharist, Penance, Anointing of the Sick, Holy Orders, and Matrimony. People sense Jesus in us and begin to want what we have and to be what we are. Maybe not consciously to begin with, but it happens sooner or later. If we reinforce this with Christ-like words, deeds and attitudes, then even the hardest of hearts will be overwhelmed by the grace of the Holy Spirit and will come to an awareness of the person of Jesus. The presence of Jesus is what evangelizes and saves people. That is why talking about Jesus and witnessing to Jesus are two different things. As Catholics, we can no longer afford to spin the Gospel and the Church and Jesus himself. The secular world does not like Catholics because we refuse to change and be conformed to their Godless agenda. The world of today hates the Church because it opposes abortion, euthanasia, same-sex marriage, etc. They ask us "why can't you give in and come with us?" Our answer is very simple: "we cannot because we are Catholic. I cannot because Jesus Christ is my Lord and Savior. I hold fast to the teachings of God's commandments and the Gospel of Jesus Christ. I cannot because I refuse to agree that because something is legal that therefore it is right. I refuse to accept abortion, euthanasia, gay marriage, etc., because they are immoral and wrong. And I will never vote for anyone who departs from these truths."

Fortitude is one of the four cardinal virtues, along with prudence, justice and temperance. We should pray for this virtue and resist the darkness of our times.

"Be sober, be watchful. Your adversary the devil prowls around like a roaring lion, seeking someone to devour. Resist him, firm in your faith, knowing that the same experience of suffering is required of your brotherhood throughout the world." (1 Peter 5:8-9)

May the power and presence of the risen Christ be with all of us in Magnificat; and remember, "we are Easter people and alleluia is our song!" (St. Augustine)

August 2013

"With the harp I will solve my problem" [Psalm 49:5]

The greatest book of poetry ever written is in the Bible. It is called the Book of Psalms. It is also the most frequently read book of poetry in the world. Tens of thousands of men and women celebrate this sacred poetry in song every day, seven times a day. Being part of the Bible it is the inspired word of God. It used to be thought that the author of the Psalms was King David, but as you can imagine it is a bit more complicated than that.

The church celebrates the Liturgy of the Hours making use of these wonderful inspired prayers which variously give expression to every emotion and movement of the human spirit, and there is nothing that does not find expression in these wonderful poems. There is an amazing description of the Psalms written by St. Ambrose which you will find in the Divine Office of Readings, Saturday of Week Ten in Ordinary Time. I could not do better than to quote some passages for you and recommend that you read the lesson from St. Ambrose for yourselves.

"A psalm is a blessing on the lips of the people, a hymn in praise of God, the assembly's homage, a general acclamation, a word that speaks for all, the voice of the Church, a confession of faith in song. It is the voice of complete assent, the joy of freedom, a cry of happiness, the echo of gladness. It soothes the temper, distracts from care, lightens the burden of sorrow. It is a source of security at night, a lesson in wisdom by day. It is a shield when we are afraid, a celebration of holiness, a vision of serenity, a promise of peace and harmony. It is like a lyre, evoking harmony from a blend of notes. Day begins to the music of a psalm. Day closes to the echo of a psalm.

In a psalm, instruction vies with beauty. We sing for pleasure. We learn for our profit. What experience is not covered by a reading of the psalms? I come across the words: A song for the beloved, and I am aflame with desire for God's love. I go through God's revelation in all its beauty, the intimations of resurrection, the gifts of his promise. I learn to avoid sin. I see my mistake in feeling ashamed of repentance for my sins."

Magnificat recommends that we celebrate Morning and Evening Prayer from the Divine Office every day. It is the prayer of the church. It is the prayer of Christ himself. It is the word of God. We lift two arms to pray the Divine Office. One is the arm of praise of God so beautifully expressed in all of the Psalms. The other is the arm of intercession for God's people and for the whole church. When you take up the Divine Office be aware that your prayer reaches to the ends of the earth, because it comes from the heart of Christ Himself.

I hope everyone is enjoying the summer and that you are finding Christ in every person and in every moment.

October 2013

October and the Rosary

I have a special feeling for the Feast of the Holy Rosary since it was the day that I was formally received into the Vincentian Community. It was the start of my vocation to be a Vincentian priest, which has brought me a life of great happiness and genuine fulfillment. I marvel at how much the Lord has blessed me, especially my apostolate of working for the priesthood.

Somehow I have experienced the Blessed Virgin Mary as having been a kind of mystical catalyst whose presence has given me a special grace of responding to Jesus and to the leading of His Holy Spirit. I like to think that this is so because of the nature of her total giving to Jesus and the will of the Father. I believe that the key to this is the gift of the Rosary, through which we are constantly experiencing the life and mysteries of her Son. In October each year the Church puts this extraordinary prayer on our lips and in our hearts as a living special grace for us "poor banished children of Eve."

The Rosary is a pure stream of grace flowing through the Immaculate Heart of Mary into the lives of her children when they say this amazing prayer. It is a school of sanctity where we learn the obedience of Mary and Jesus without which it is impossible for us to become holy. The Rosary is the bond which binds us to Christ and to the Church. It is the golden chain that reveals us as willing servants of our Blessed Mother. It is the song book of the poor from which we sing the praise of Jesus in the different ages of His life with us. It is Mary's home school where she "teaches us" how to be like her Beloved Son.

May the Blessed Mother of Jesus, Queen of the Most Holy Rosary, leave the door open and the light on for all of us.

"Somehow I have experienced the Blessed Virgin Mary as having been a kind of mystical catalyst whose presence has given me a special grace of responding to Jesus and to the leading of His Holy Spirit."

December 2013

Say A Prayer for Me

When I worked in England as a young priest after my ordination, I met a lot of lapsed Catholics who would invariably say to me, "I don't go to church no more. I think Catholics are just a lot of hypocrites. They go to Mass on Sunday and then go straight to the pub." My answer which always disarmed them was, "And what's wrong with going to the pub?" I should explain that whereas in the U.S. people go to bars to drink, in England and Ireland they go to pubs to talk. For my Yorkshire friends, however, pubs and religion shouldn't be mixed; which of course is ridiculous.

Some people can always find their own excuses for leaving the Church. The truth is never as simple as what people try to make it out. You can blame Father Jack or Sister Jill, or whoever you want, or you can disagree with Church teaching and discipline, etcetera, etcetera. The fact is that to leave the Church is to turn your back on Jesus Christ. Jesus is the sole reason why we go to Church on Sundays. We go to Mass, "Do this in memory of Me," to worship God the Father through His Son Jesus in the Holy Spirit.

Apart from this, there is a great deal of dishonesty, perversity and hypocrisy in the hearts of many who "leave the Church." It seems now that any old excuse will do. For them, Jesus has become a real inconvenience in their chosen life of egoism and self-will. And this is why Jesus, through the Church, is right to call us to repent. Repentance is always the key that lets us back into the Church. There are two kinds of people who leave the Church: those who do not know any better and who we need to evangelize, and those who simply "will not serve." Many of them have been well instructed in the faith and are infected with the modern viruses of disobedience and arrogance. People like these need to "humble themselves before the mighty hand of God (1 Peter 5:6)." They need to put their pride in their pocket and repent. Such repentance is best expressed in the Sacrament of Reconciliation. I once heard an English Bishop who had a lot of pastoral experience say, "You know, death bed conversions are few. Most people die the way they live. If they live in the awareness of God, they will die in the awareness of God. Otherwise, they may meet God as a stranger." Thank God that His mercy will always far exceed our repentance.

Our Lady of Medjugorje asked the visionaries to pray one Hail Mary for the conversion of sinners. She once took Jakov to China and showed him an old man who lay dying and she said, "This man has lived a very evil life, but because of your Hail Mary, Jesus is taking him to heaven this day.

Some years ago one of my Vincentian Confreres, a well-known charismatic priest in Ireland, announced one morning in the month of June that Charlie Chaplin would die on Christmas day. He said, "I must pray for him." And sure enough, six months later on Christmas day the little man died and I am sure went to his reward.

For months before Sammy Davis Jr. died, the Lord put him in my heart to pray for him every day, which I did. I learned afterwards that he needed a lot of prayers, and I am looking forward to meeting him in heaven and having a chat.

And finally, on a lighter note, during my second year in England, I visited the house of a good practicing English Catholic and his family. I asked him, "Are there any other Catholics living on your street." The man said, "There is an Irishman living six doors from here, but you will only be wasting your time asking him to go back to Church." I said, "Well, we'll have to see about that." The man said, "Father, I will bet you ten pounds that you will not get him to go back to Mass." I went to see the Irishman, and introduced myself and said, "There is an Englishman who bet me ten pounds that I will not persuade you to return to Sunday Mass." He replied, "Did he say that now?"

Next Sunday, he was at Mass and he came to see me afterwards and said, "You know Father, I think maybe I should go to confession. Have you a moment?" Weeks later, he asked me, "Tell me Father, did you ever get the ten pounds?" I said, "I did indeed." "I am glad," he replied. Then he said, "You know Father, that man did me a very great favor. God bless him."

God is constantly putting people into our minds and onto our hearts. People we had not thought of for years, and people we pass on the street or see at the checkout, or remember during Mass. We should always pray for them, that they will be saved. No prayer is too short. And as we all know, prayer reaches to the ends of the earth.

We of Magnificat should never lose an opportunity to pray for our country, for our friends, and for the many strangers in our midst, that the Lord will pour out His Mercy on us all. God bless you.

March 2014

In the Breaking of Bread
[Luke 24:30]

When I was in the seminary, my professor of speech and homiletics had never preached a retreat and knew little about homiletics, and I learned everything I needed to know about voice production in two minutes from an actor from the Abbey Theater. In those days, priesthood was a qualification that fitted everything. His direction to us was to type out your homily, learn it by heart, and deliver it like a Victorian Shakespearian actor. I did this, not the actor however, for my first six months after ordination until one Sunday morning after two sentences, I forgot my text and was faced with one of those "what do I do now" moments. Do I come down in shame or continue brazenly? I decided on the latter course, and proceeded to give a really dreadful homily. After Mass I was skulking my way out of the church when at the door a young man came over to me and said, "Father, I have never heard such a homily in all my life." I was wondering what he meant by that, when he added, "Your words have moved me to tears. Would you kindly hear my confession?" It was not what I expected. It did teach me however an important lesson about the ordained ministry and the proclamation of the Word of God; namely, that it is Jesus who speaks through us.

Recently, while reading paragraph 7 of the "Vatican Council: Constitution on the Sacred Liturgy" I was struck again on how beautifully the paragraph describes the various presences of Jesus during the celebration of the Holy Eucharist: how He is present in the Word proclaimed during the liturgy, how He is present uniquely in the Sacred Species which we receive at Communion, how He is present in his people gathered together in His name, and how He is present in the person of the priest. During the celebration of the Eucharist over the last few weeks, the Lord gave me a spiritual inspiration concerning His presence at Mass, and that, given the opportunity, I ought to speak about it more often. As a result of this, I wrote the following prayer/poem:

"I Know That It Is You"

Lord, You are at the door to greet me; that feeling
I get is You.
I know that it is You.

Your prayer lifts me.
I hear Your presence
in the Word proclaimed.
I know that it is You.

And when I offer your peace
to those around me,
it is You who catch my eye.
I know that it is You.

And the bread that is not bread,
and the wine that is not wine,
now Your Paschal self;
fresh from supper table,
Holy Cross and empty tomb.
I know that it is You.

You bless me
with the hands of your priest
and send me forth;
no longer me,
but You in me.
I know that it is You.

[cf. Vatican Council: Constitution on the Sacred Liturgy #7]

I hope you like it and I hope you will feel free to use and reproduce it, but not change it. We in Magnificat should become more and more aware of everything that will help us to come to a deeper understanding of the mystery of Christ's presence in the Sacred Liturgy, and particularly the sacraments. What the Vatican Council teaches about the presence of Jesus during the Eucharist has brought us to a more profound understanding of this central mystery of our faith. May I wish you every blessing during this year, and especially during the holy season of Lent and Easter.

PS. May I recommend the following books:

Dangers to the Faith: Recognizing Catholicism's 21st Century Opponents by Al Kresta published by Our Sunday Visitor

A Prayer Journal by Flannery O'Connor published by MacmillanUSA

"You must always come to Me so that I may come to you."

Saint John XXIII

I was still in the seminary when John XXIII was elected in October 1958. Our director came to tell us the news that Angelo Roncalli had been elected Pope, a seventy-eight year old Cardinal whom no one had ever heard of. Our director had just returned from Rome with his doctorate in Canon Law under his arm. Pius XII had been Pope: a giant and a saint. The director stood ashen-faced before us telling us that Roncalli had been elected, and then he added, uncharacteristically for him: "I don't think the Holy Spirit had much to do with this." Within a week, Pope Pius XII was forgotten and this little rotund smiling man was winning the whole world by his wit and joy.

The Cardinals who elected him would have considered him, to use a football idiom, "a safe pair of hands" who would surely do nothing to rock the barque of Peter. Pope John was probably thinking "well have I got news for you." What did he do? Out of the blue he called an Ecumenical Council, now known to us as Vatican II. All the Cardinals in the Vatican and many outside thought this little new Pope had lost the run of himself. By academic training Pope John was an historian. He had acquired a doctorate in church history as a young priest, so he knew a lot about how the Church had faired down the ages. It would have been hard to shock or surprise him.

In his meetings with the Cardinals in preparation for the Council he observed a lot of heated exchanges. When this occurred, instead of offering a solution, he would begin to talk about his father who was a farmer in Bergamo. His observations about sowing seeds and patiently waiting seemed to diffuse many debates and brought people back to quietness and to an acceptance of other people's view points. Many stories have been told about him. Once when someone asked him how many people worked in the Vatican, he answered "about half." But shortly after that, he decided to double their wages. I remember after his election how he found a sweater which his priest's secretary from Bergamo had left behind. The Pope sent it to him with a note: "in the cold of Bergamo, you will need this more than I do." I read another story in a newspaper around the same time about an Anglican (Episcopal) priest who left his new Latin breviary in St. Peters. He wrote to the administrator there, who gave the letter to Pope John, and guess what he did? He wrote to the priest and sent him the four volumes of his own breviary with a note asking the priest to pray for the Pope.

What I have learned from Pope John is that life is essentially about becoming a saint, becoming holy. You see this in his book "Journal of a Soul." As Papal Nuncio in Eastern Europe, he helped all the poor people who came to see him, and enabled many Jewish people to escape to safety and freedom. Indeed he and Pope John Paul II have brought about an extraordinary healing between Christians and Jews. When Pope John saw a need, he did something. When he saw a needy person, he never asked any questions. Saints act like this, and Pope John taught us that real Christ-like holiness should permeate everything we do, every moment of our lives. Let us pray then to Saint John XXIII and ask him to intercede for the Church, for Magnificat, and for the whole world. Amen.

September 2014

Brother Bo and Sir Felix:

I had an occasion recently to observe the behavior of a seeing-eye-dog, which prompted an aimless reflection on dogs and cats. So, at the risk of sounding like Andy Rooney, I beg you to bear with me a little.

The dog in question was some kind of lab, the essence of gentleness, the obedience of a Jesuit, and the patience of Mother Teresa. "Dogs", I thought, "are noble animals." Their only aim in life is to please their owner. Dogs will welcome you home with obvious gestures of delight, overpowering at times. They will sit and look at you, as if to say, "Is there anything I can do for you?" Some dogs will bring you your slippers, or the newspaper or car keys, depending on what he thinks you need. Outdoors he will fetch you a stick and invite you to throw it. And if you do, he will run off and bring it back. Even if you throw it in a lake, he will jump in, swim out, grab the stick, swim back, shake himself off and invite you to do it all over again. A dog will go up a mountain and round-up a couple hundred sheep and direct them to a field with just a few whistles from his master. He will guard your children. I once saw a dog grab a doctor gently by the wrist when he was about to give an injection to a little girl. He only let go when the mother entered the room and had indicated that everything was okay. All in all, the dog is a "rather good fellow," though of course not all of them are saints.

The cat, on the other hand, is different. His world revolves around himself. If he bothers to welcome your return home, it is with mincing step, curved back and a raised tail. His body language says, "How do I look?" and his upturned gaze says, "What have you for me today?" None of the leaping, shirt-staining, slobbery, face-licking welcome of Brother Bo, but rather the narcissistic soft-shoe tread of Sir Felix himself. If Sir Felix ever dared to accompany you out of doors, there would be no cavorting up mountains. And if you threw a stick into the water, he would sit and watch, thinking "If he thinks

I am going into the water to fetch that dumb stick, he better think again." In the face of real danger, a dog will defend you to the death where as a cat will scramble up the nearest tree.

So really, dogs are saints. They love it when we are good, and they are embarrassed when we are bad. But still they love us. It is not recorded whether St. Paul had a dog, but I bet he liked them. His list of virtues and gifts, especially 1 Cor. 13:4, fits dogs perfectly. They are patient and loving, not a bit jealous, arrogant or rude. They know how to rejoice with us and they are not posh or proud, like some animals I could mention. Dogs are good sufferers. They never complain, and they can grieve when sad things happen. I am sure that there are dogs in heaven. One old lady, when asked responded, "if there are no dogs in heaven, I ain't goin."

So observe your dog. He is your best creaturely friend who on any given day will show you the way to perfection. And to those of you who are proud cat owners, you are probably furious with me. If you are, do not write to me or email me. It's just summer. Enjoy it. I love cats too.

I saw a t-shirt recently worn by a priest. It read "Jesus loves you. But I'm his favorite." I have not seen a cat wearing this t-shirt—yet.

God bless you all,
Fr. Kevin, C.M.

December 2014

St. Catherine of Genoa on Purgatory

It is a bit late in November to talk about Purgatory or the need to pray for the Holy Souls. However, I do so because I recently read an amazingly beautiful and consoling Treatise on Purgatory written by St. Catherine of Genoa. I had never read it before and came across it while surfing the web, iPieta to be precise.

Catherine of Genoa was a 15th Century mystic of a noble Italian family who became a Canoness of St. Augustine. During her life she had a profoundly mystical encounter with Our Lord Jesus. It was in one of these mystical ecstasies that Jesus revealed to her the state of souls in Purgatory. It is fascinating to read this work in which the Lord allowed her to have insights into Purgatory and how it is experienced by the Holy Souls. I will quote here from the fifth chapter to give you a flavor of St. Catherine's mystical insights. Keep in mind that what she has written is not holy writ, but a private revelation. The fact that it is the experience of such a great mystical daughter of the Church, who is a canonized Saint, gives it a credence that it might not otherwise have.

So here is what she has written in Chapter 5:

The souls in Purgatory have wills accordant in all things with the will of God, who therefore sheds on them His goodness, and they, as far as their will goes, are happy and cleansed of all their sin. As for guilt, these cleansed souls are as they were when God created them, for God forgives their guilt immediately who have passed from this life ill content with their sins, having confessed all they have committed and having the will to commit no more. Only the rust of sin is left them and from this they cleanse themselves by pain in the fire. Thus cleansed of all guilt and united in will to God, they see Him clearly in the degree in which He makes Himself known to them, and see too how much it imports to enjoy Him and that souls have been created for this end. Moreover, they are brought to so uniting a conformity with God, and are drawn to Him in such wise, His natural instinct towards souls working in them, that neither arguments nor figures nor examples can make the thing clear as the mind knows it to be in effect and as by inner feeling it is understood to be. I will, however, make one comparison which comes to my mind.

I would recommend that you read this Treatise in its entirety which you can easily google. If you can, you should acquire the app "iPieta" which contains many of the great spiritual classics as well as a plethora of other things that will amaze you.

St. Catherine's writing on Purgatory I find to be very enlightening and very consoling. As for the increasing number of people now-a-days who deny the existence of Purgatory, it would be a good thing to remind them that the existence of Purgatory is a defined dogma of our faith; to deny it therefore would make one a heretic.

May the Lord grant you a blessed Advent, a mystical Christmas, and growth in holiness in 2015. I will be praying for you and offering the Holy Eucharist for you on Christmas morning.

God bless you all,
Fr. Kevin, C.M.

March 2015

Paul VI: Pope and Prophet

I arrived to study at Catholic University on the day that Humanae Vitae was published by Pope Paul VI in 1968. The following day a meeting was called of resident theologians to discuss this new encyclical, and I thought it was important enough for me to attend. What I was not expecting was the intensity of the feelings that were expressed against what the Pope had written. Afterwards, when I left the auditorium, an undergraduate girl came up to me carrying a large picture of the Pope. Standing in front of me, she said, "This is what I think of the Pope," and proceeded to tear the picture into small pieces, throwing them into the air. This was my first introduction to the controversy surrounding Humanae Vitae.

The years have passed and in the intervening time, the dire warnings, given by Pope Paul about the effects of widespread contraception, have proven to be accurate. We have only to look around and observe the bitter fruits of contraception and the effect it is having on family life. In the last weeks Pope Francis has intimated his intention of beatifying Pope Paul VI. In doing this, he is performing a symbolic gesture and giving the Church's unqualified approval of the Papal Ministry of this holy man and his teaching. Pope Paul did not initiate the Second Vatican Council; that was the inspiration of St. John XXIII. His task was to preside over it, which caused him great suffering. His vigilance and wisdom has been acknowledged by almost everyone in the Church, and without him, things might have been much different.

Many of us remember how devotion to the Blessed Virgin Mary was affected by the Council. People felt that saying the Rosary, along with many other devotions, was not important any more, now that the liturgy had been restored. In response to this, Pope Paul wrote the most beautiful encyclical Marialis Cultus, insisting on the importance for Catholics of expressions of devotion to Mary, the Mother of God. Being aware of the crisis in the priesthood generated by Vatican II, he wrote an encyclical on the theology of the priesthood and another one on the Blessed Eucharist. In the meantime, he was facing considerable opposition from many people, even bishops and priests throughout the Church, who seemed to be disagreeing with him and dissenting from his teaching. This caused him great pain, and yet his mind was reaching out to the ends of the earth. He became the first pope to escape the confines of the Vatican when he visited the Holy Land and the Philippines.

The fortitude of this man underscores the need for pastors and all the baptized to be faithful to the teaching of the Gospel and the Magisterium of the Church. Pope Paul knew that many theologians were in favor of the availability of contraception. But he, led by the Spirit, decided differently. He allowed himself to be guided by the light of the Holy Spirit and the truth of Jesus Christ.

Today, Pope Francis is faced with a similar dilemma at the coming Synod in October of this year. It will be his task to gather up the wisdom of the theologians, and the prayerful reflection of his fellow bishops, and decide on behalf of the Church what we are to believe and how we are to act regarding the moral issues being discussed at the Synod. The same dilemma faces each and every one of us. Are we going to be taught by the secular world, with its absolute relativism [do it yourself morality], or are we going to be enlightened by Christ and by the teaching of His Holy Church.

I have been asked to compose a prayer for the Synod, which you will find on my website: www.intercessionforpriests.org. Please feel free to download and use as you wish. I look forward to seeing many of you at the Magnificat Conference in Washington, DC. In the meantime, we must pray much for the Holy Father and for the Synod.

God Bless You!
Fr. Kevin C.M.

A PRAYER for the SYNOD of BISHOPS on the FAMILY

Loving Father,
Creator of Heaven and Earth,
through Your Son, Our Lord Jesus Christ,
You teach us what to believe and how to live.
Look upon Your Church in our struggle
against the powers of darkness and deceit.
Guide our Holy Father and the Bishops
by the light of Your Spirit,
as they prepare for the coming Synod.
Inspire them to bring an end to confusion
and proclaim the truth concerning
human life, human sexuality, and
the true meaning of marriage and family.
We make this prayer through Christ,
our Lord. Amen.

August 2015

You Must Always Come To Me

The Basilica di Sant'Andrea delle Fratte is a little church tucked away in the corner over from the Piazza di Spagna. It is quite a famous church having several of Bernini's sculptures and other pieces. It was at this side altar that Saint Maximilian Kolbe celebrated his first mass and where Our Lady of the Miraculous Medal appeared to Alphonse Ratisbonne, a Jewish man who converted to the faith and founded religious communities to promote relations between Jews and Catholics. It was also featured in Puccini's opera Tosca.

While staying in Rome I would often go there to pray and attend Mass, and sometimes go to confession. Because of demand and the number of priests who wish to celebrate at St. Maximilian's altar, there is normally a Mass every half hour. Sr. Briege and I were asked to speak at the Mass for the closing of The Year for Priests. The day before I decided to go there to confession. My plan was to attend the ongoing Mass, make my confession, and assist at the next Mass.

When I was going into the church I was preceded by a little man carrying a backpack. He went into a pew and I went into the pew across the aisle from him. As I did this, he turned to me, smiled and bowed. Slightly puzzled I began my preparation for confession while the Mass was proceeding. I did not pay much attention to the Mass, intending to receive communion at the following Mass. Suddenly, as from nowhere, the man appeared before me with his outstretched hand holding the Sacred Host. Taken aback, I tried to indicate that he should receive; that the Host was for him and not me. At this he leaned reverently forward and said to me in very clear English, "No, this is not for me, this is for you," and he placed the Sacred Host in my hand and I consumed it. Meanwhile, there was a person standing near with hands folded in an attitude of great reverence, who, when I received the Host, bowed and seemed to move away. The man then left the church at once.

Still somewhat stunned, I went and asked a priest to hear my confession at which point I learned that there would not be another Mass that morning. So I decided to sit for a while, reflecting on this unusual but deeply touching experience. I said, "Lord, please explain to me what just happened here." At once, an inner voice said to me, "You must always come to Me so that I may come to you." I had never heard Holy Communion being expressed in such a manner. After an intense period of meditation on all of this, I made my way back to the convent where I was staying.

As I walked I began to think of this man. He was not too tall with brown short cut hair, brown beard, and deep brown eyes. I thought to myself "I know this man" and several names came into my mind: Padre Pio, St. John Vianney, and St. Francis. As I passed the statue of the Immaculate Conception in the Piazza di Spagna, one name came clearly and with certainty into my mind, Blessed Charles de Foucauld. It was a real epiphany. The little man was Blessed Charles de Foucauld. The attending reverent person, was this an accompanying angel to protect the Holy Eucharist and to adore Jesus?

When Jesus said, " You must always come to me so that I may come to you," He was expressing an important truth of our faith and of our sacramental life. Until then I had never been aware of the joy we give Jesus when He comes to us in the Holy Eucharist. It was a new revelation. We see today how many receive Jesus very casually and maybe even unworthily. Jesus was expressing his delight at being received with reverence and welcome. It was as if He was saying, "Thank you for your welcome. Thank you for providing Me a place where I can feel at home, where I can rest and find love and peace."

This experience burned in my heart with great intensity and still returns to me from time to time. With an experience like this there is often a residue of doubt about it's authenticity. Some months later, Sr. Briege and I were conducting a retreat for priests in England, and during that retreat this experience kept coming into my mind. I prayed, "Jesus I hope You do not mind, but I am going to lay a fleece before You. I will take Your answer and give You thanks." The fleece that I put before the Lord is that I would meet a priest that day named Charles. So I finished my prayer and got on with my work.

When it came for the time for me to celebrate the Sacrament of Reconciliation, I went to the room and prepared for the first penitent. In due course, the door opened and a young priest came in and said, "Good morning Father Kevin. My name is Fr. Charlie." I smiled and said to myself, "Thank You, Lord."

All of this has transformed the way that I approach Holy Communion and I hope that those who read this will experience the love and nearness of our Eucharistic Lord.

*Jesus WiFi,
password: Come
Holy Spirit*

October 2015

JESUS WIFI
PASSWORD: COME HOLY SPIRIT

I write in the aftermath of the Pope's visit to the U.S. By any standard, it was a triumph, a tsunami of Divine Grace, a unique moment in U.S. history. The American people do not realize yet how their country has been changed. The tyranny of secularism has been breached. And the Pope is right in suggesting that the worst aspect of environmental abuse is the treatment of poor people and their children. We all know that when the IMF and the World Bank discuss loans for the Third World, their first suggestion is to kill unborn children and to sterilize their mothers. The greatest treasure of the poor is their children, and Pope Francis would say "feed them, don't kill them." People, especially T.V. people, kept asking, "What is it about this Pope? What is this magnetism; where is it coming from?" We all have our smartphones. We are familiar with that feeling of trying to get something where there is no WiFi, so you can't read Zenit or Drudge, or anything else because there is no WiFi. Pope Francis is like a gigantic WiFi transmitter. And the transmitter is called Jesus. We receive this beautiful clear signal through our special receptor which we call Baptism: not by means of Google, but by means of the Holy Spirit. This is my simple explanation of what happens. Like all analogies, it is limited. But when people are looking at and listening to Pope Francis, they are looking at and listening to Jesus. Baptized Catholics know this with a certainty of faith. They who are not baptized are also aware of being in the presence of the God who loves us all. Pope Francis said to them, "If you can't send me your prayers, then send me your goodwill and good wishes."

People say, he should have used the word abortion. He did not, because he was aware that for any woman listening to him who had procured an abortion, the sound of that word would have been like a dagger driven into her heart. When the "sinful woman" was brought before Jesus, He did not scold her for being a sinner, nor did He tell her that she had not sinned. She knew that she had. He told her, lovingly, that no one had condemned her and that He did not condemn her either. And then He said, "Go now and sin no more" (John 8:1-11).

Pope Francis is not going to change the truth of the Church's teaching on anything. He can't. He is the Pope. What he is trying to do is to invent a new way of expressing such teaching: a way that is loving and reconciling, and a way that does not condemn. He realizes that there is enough harshness and negativity in this world. I hear people criticizing him because he says things differently. It is the age of mercy, and the Jubilee Year of Mercy begins on the Feast of the Immaculate Conception. May we who belong to Magnificat show the merciful face of Jesus to all the banished children of Eve.

December 2015

Vocation to a Consecrated Life

The vocation to Consecrated Virginity has existed since the early church and is the oldest form of consecration in the church. It pre-dates the emergence of religious life. Mention is made of this vocation in the early church by people like Saint Ignatius of Antioch, Saint Ciprian, St. Ambrose and others: examples abound, such as Saint Agnes, Saint Agatha, Saint Cecilia, Saint Lucy and Saint Catherine. Even Saint Patrick in his autobiography The Confession commented on the great number of young Irish women who, in response to his preaching, embraced the state of virginity for the sake of Christ and the service of the Gospel. In those early times, the consecration was not a form of religious life characterized by the taking of religious vows. These were single lay women living in the world and serving the church by a life of prayer while involved in various apostolates under the direction of the bishop. The vocation of consecrated virgins living in the world was not really made clear until its revival at the Second Vatican Council and in 1983 when it was incorporated into the Code of Canon Law #604. The church was to establish this form of consecration as a vocation for women to follow a way of life which would be recognized and accepted by the Bishop as an integral part of the life of his diocese.

My own experience of dealing with women who came to me wanting to embrace this way was to get the church involved by introducing them to their local priest and bishop. Unfortunately, I found that both bishops and priests were simply not interested. But things have changed in the last number of years, and now bishops have a more informed view of things, especially as more and more women are coming forward. Such as vocation requires mature discernment. This is usually done by the pastor or spiritual director and ultimately by the bishop himself. He is the one who discerns and decides how to go forward, and how long the period of probation ought to last. My own view is that, with the demise of so many religious communities and the emergence of new ones, it seems providential that, guided by the Holy Spirit, the church would provide for people who do not wish to be religious but who desire to live a consecrated life in the service of the church. Those I have guided to enter into such a consecration have experienced a profound transformation in their inner lives, and also in their apostolate within the church. I know that there are many women today who are looking for just such a way to dedicate their lives to Christ. Those who came to me had already been living deeply spiritual sacramental lives, which is part of the requirement of undertaking such a consecration. I am sure that there are many single women and widows out there who would gladly consecrate themselves to Jesus Christ and to a life of holiness of body and soul.

May all of us in Magnificat pray earnestly that these wonderful virtues, proclaimed by the Church in every age, would continue to flourish in the Church. I pray that our Blessed Mother Mary would draw many people to follow her under her banner of Queen of Virgins. I wish you every grace and blessing in this Season of Advent and the Birth of Our Savior, Jesus Christ.

March 2016

Living in the Shadow of the Cross

When Jesus told the Apostles that he must go up to Jerusalem, and be rejected by the high priests and people and be put to death, he was admonished by Peter who said, "Lord, nothing of the kind is ever going to happen to you." Dietrich Bonhoeffer commenting on this passage said that even the apostles wanted a Christ without suffering, without the cross. Even though Jesus had explicitly told them that unless they were going to take up the cross daily and follow him, they could not be his disciples. The central action of the redemptive work of Jesus was performed when he breathed his last and died hanging on the cross.

In the past, the cross was frequently mentioned as an integral part of our lives in Christ. People had no problem with it because they could see that everybody suffered something or other, sooner or later.

The mysticism of the cross is seldom mentioned in the Church of the 21st century, and there seems to be an expectation that no one, young or old, should ever have to suffer anything. The truth is that the doctrine of the cross is essential to the Christian life: it was for Jesus who was lifted up on the cross, it was for Mary who stood beneath the cross of her son and watched him die a terrible death, and it was for the saints known and unknown who experienced strength through their embrace of the cross of Christ in their own lives. St. Paul wrote, "I make up in my body what is wanted to the sufferings of Christ." In reality, the cross is the only thing that gives meaning to human suffering, because it changes human misery and pain into peace and joy. The ultimate healing is that of being able to embrace and kiss the wood of the cross because all healing comes to us through the sacrifice which Jesus offered on the cross. "By his wounds we are healed" (Isaiah 53:5). Human life brings its share of anger, bitterness, resentment, fear, withdrawal, timidity, anxiety and guilt. These afflictions of fallen human nature can be healed, but only when we transform them into meekness, humility, acceptance, and fortitude, etcetera. The healing of the cross for us Catholics comes to us primarily in the Eucharist: "Say but the word, and I shall be healed." The Eucharistic sacrifice of Christ is augmented for us in Eucharistic adoration and devotion to the Blessed Sacrament, and wonderfully in the Sacraments of Reconciliation and of the Anointing of the Sick.

Jim Murphy, a fine Catholic man, was inspired one year to carry a large wooden cross all the way across the United States. He told of many encounters he had, and of healings he had witnessed. One that stands out happened when he was walking on a lonely road somewhere in the deep South carrying his cross. A car passed him going in his direction, and a couple of hundred yards further on screeched to a stop. When Jim came up to the car he saw the driver kneeling in tears by the open door. Jim stopped and waited. Eventually, the man spoke. He said, "You know sir, I have been a Baptist minister in this area for nearly forty years, and in all of that time I have never preached on the cross of Jesus. I see now, and I was wrong and regret it very much."

For those of us who are baptized into Christ Jesus, who are tabernacles of the Most Blessed Trinity, there must never be any fear of the cross of Christ. It is not simply bitterness and pain. It is in truth, the joy of the Lord, the peace of Christ, and the anointing of the Holy Spirit. I have known so many people who in spite of great suffering were radiant with the presence and holiness of Jesus Christ.

Finally, the devotion of making the Stations of the Cross has virtually disappeared from the devotional lives of Catholics. We in Magnificat should try to rediscover this beautiful Catholic practice.

May the Lord continue to bless all of you during this Season of Lent, and prepare your hearts for the great celebration of the Paschal Mystery.

September 2016

Is Anyone Sick Among You? [James 5:14]

My late sister Josie had an unusual charism. She felt drawn by the Lord to minister to the spiritual needs of those who were sick, especially if they were drawing near to death. In the small community in which we grew up, she knew them all by their first names. She would visit them in their homes at a time convenient for the family, bringing with her a blessed candle, holy water, medals, and perhaps a little statue of Our Lady or the Sacred Heart. On one occasion, I watched her talk to the family about the sick person. She would then go to the person in question, and speak with them and begin to pray, always familiar prayers, and the sick person would join in or just listen. In those days people seldom went to the hospital. They remained at home and, more often than not, would die there. Families were glad to see her. It helped to ease their burden.

Lately, I have come to observe that these customs surrounding sickness and the onset of death have almost entirely disappeared as people have become more secularized and estranged from the Church and from their faith. This has resulted in a situation where people who are physically well cared for are spiritually neglected. Sick people want and need people to help them to keep in touch with God. I have noticed that people hardly ever send for the priest, thereby depriving their loved ones of the great graces that come through Confession, the Anointing of the Sick, and especially the Holy Eucharist.

This is a real sin of omission and neglect. It means that poor sick people, at the moment of their greatest need, are unable to experience these saving encounters with their Lord and Savior. For some years I have thought of a way to fill this gap in the devotional lives of those who are dying and those who are caring for them. So I wrote a little book of prayers and meditations to help people to pray for those waiting for the Lord to return, to put oil in their lamps as it were. The book is titled "Is Anyone Sick Among You" [James 5:14]. It is published by Amazon in the U.S., and by Veritas in Ireland.

I mention it to you of Magnificat because of the wide circle of people whom you encounter who may from time to time need help from such a book.

Visiting the sick is one of the seven Corporal Works of Mercy. St. Teresa of Calcutta constantly reminded her sisters, and all of us, that when we minister to the sick we are ministering to Christ himself. In these times when the value of human life is being constantly diminished, it is good for us to remember that when we lay our hands on the sick and look into their eyes, we are laying our hands on the person of Jesus and looking into His eyes.

May the Lord continue to bless all of you.

December 2016

In these times, the President and Members of Congress, and all those involved in government are surely in need of our fervent prayers. Someone asked me to write a prayer for the Country, I did so and this is it:

A Prayer for the United States
Lord God, Father of all Your children,
we thank You for our homeland,
the United States of America,
and for our Constitutional Democracy.
Send Your Holy Spirit to enlighten our President
and those who serve us in Congress.
Bless all who draft our laws,
and the men and women who administer them.
Look with mercy on us your children
who cry out to you.
May your truth dispel all moral darkness.
Protect life and family,
and help us to live in peace.
We make this prayer
through Christ our Lord. Amen.
Our Lady of the Immaculate Conception; pray for us.
Saints of the Americas; pray for us.

"You are a slave of no one except God, so behave like free people and never use your freedom as a cover for wickedness. Have respect for everyone and love for your fellow believers, fear God and honor the Emperor." 1 Peter 2:16-17

I wish you many blessings for this beautiful Season of Advent and great peace this Christmas and throughout the coming year. Please pray for me.

"Say but the word, and I shall be healed." Jesus Christ is present in His word. He points the way. He is the Truth. He gives us life.

March 2017

L ent is upon us again, a liturgical season which is poorly understood by many people, particularly when it comes to the requirement of fasting. The authoritative Papal document on the church's teaching on penance was written by Blessed Pope Paul VI in his famous Apostolic Constitution called 'Paenitemini.' I have found that people know little of what is required in terms of Christian penance, so I include for your benefit the appropriate text found in Chapter three of 'Paenitemini.' May I suggest that this document be read by all of us in Magnificat because it is a beautiful presentation of the Church's understanding concerning the age old tradition of fasting. The document is short, but a real gem coming from the pen of this saintly Pope, Blessed Paul VI.

Here is the relevant passage from the document concerning the Church's understanding of fast and abstinence:

By divine law all the faithful are required to do penance. The prescriptions of Church law regarding penance are totally reorganized according to the following norms:

- The time of Lent preserves its penitential character. The days of penance to be observed under obligation throughout the Church are all Fridays and Ash Wednesday. With regard to the manner of fulfilling the precept of penitence on such days, abstinence is to be observed on every Friday which does not fall on a day of obligation, while abstinence and fast are to be observed on Ash Wednesday and on Good Friday.

- The law of abstinence forbids the use of meat, but not of eggs, the products of milk or condiments made of animal fat.

- The law of fasting allows only one full meal a day, but does not prohibit taking some food in the morning and evening, observing, as far as quantity and quality are concerned, approved local custom.

- To the law of abstinence those are bound who have completed their 14th year of age. To the law of fast those of the faithful are bound who have completed their 21st year and up until the beginning of their 60th year.

- As regards those of a lesser age, pastors of souls and parents should see to it with particular care that they are educated to a true sense of penitence.

The spirit of Lent is described in the Gospel for Ash Wednesday [Matthew 6:1–18] when Jesus, in addition to the practice of fasting and abstinence, refers to the giving of alms and to prayer. Many parishes throughout the world provide each home with a charity box where family members are encouraged to make financial sacrifices for the benefit of the poor. The monies collected are given to the parish at the end of Lent for that purpose. So this Gospel teaches us the principle elements of Christian penitential practice. In the reading from Isaiah 58:1-9 on the Friday after Ash Wednesday, we have the passage entitled "Is this not the sort of fast that pleases me?" where the prophet describes the many things we ought to do if our fasting is to be pleasing in the sight of God. It is interesting that in places where Our Lady has appeared, she asks us not only to pray and repent, but also to fast. Many of us can attest to the spiritual fruits brought about by this ancient practice of the Church.

Let me finish with this quote from Blessed Pope Paul VI: "Penance therefore—already in the Old Testament—is a religious, personal act which has as its aim love and surrender to God: fasting for the sake of God, not for one's own self. Such it must remain also in the various penitential rites sanctioned by law. When this is not verified, the Lord is displeased with His people: " Today you have not fasted in a way which will make your voice heard on high .... Rend your heart and not your garments, and return to the Lord your God." The social aspect of penitence is not lacking in the Old Testament. In fact, the penitential liturgies of the Old Covenant are not only a collective awareness of sin but constitute in reality a condition for belonging to the people of God. We can further establish that penitence was represented even before Christ as a means and a sign of perfection and sanctity."

May the Lord bless you during this Lent and fill you with joy when Easter comes.

Say a Prayer for Me, Father

"Say a prayer for me, Father" is a request commonly made by people to a priest; and if I say to someone "I will pray for you," even though they may not be strong believers, they are always delighted.

How often our Blessed Mother has called upon her children to pray for sinners, for the Church, for peace and reconciliation, and for the whole world. The prayer that she loves us to pray is the Holy Rosary. In the Gospels, Jesus frequently urges us to pray. He says, "you must always pray" (Luke 18:1), and "pray so that you will not fall into temptation" (Matthew 26:41). He teaches us to pray the Our Father. He says, "Ask the Lord of the harvest … to send out laborers into his harvest" (Luke 10:2). To Peter, he said, " I have prayed for you … that your faith may not fail" (Luke 22:32). Jesus encourages us to pray and not to grow weary; "Ask and you shall receive; seek and you will find; knock and the door will be opened to you" (Matthew 7:7).

Why should we ask God for things He already knows we need? It is something of a puzzle as to why it should be necessary. Perhaps it is because that is what children do when they want something. Cardinal Ratzinger says that we pray for what can only be given to us. In my life and in my priestly ministry that has always been the case. So, as God's people baptized into Jesus Christ indwelt by the Holy Trinity, we must always live in this humble attitude of prayer.

There are obvious things we should pray for relating to our lives. We pray for our spouse, for our children, our financial situation, our friends, and neighbors, etc. We must also pray for the world which is so rapidly turning away from God's revealed truth; so we have to pray for the Church, the Pope, the bishops, and clergy, that they may be holy and faithful to the teachings of the Gospel. We pray for a return to the morality of the Bible. We pray for respect for life and family and society.

Mankind has taken upon itself to redefine marriage and the family, and sexual orientation, and has set aside the biblical teaching found in the first chapters of the Book of Genesis.

Man has arrogated to himself to say who shall live and who shall not live. Sometimes it seems that there is nothing we can do about any of this. But there is. We can come before the Lord and pray and plead and intercede.

On my first visit to Medjugorje, I asked our Blessed Mother a question about my future through one of the visionaries, Marija Pavlovic. The answer I got back through Maria was simple and direct; "Tell him that all his questions will be answered in prayer."

Our prayer should reach out into the heart of the Church and the whole world, and not simply be focused on our personal needs. We should always remember that the Holy Spirit, in guiding the interior life of the Church, has inspired a significant part of the body of the Church to be devoted ceaselessly to prayer. Religious life is that special vocation given to many men and women in the Church by which they dedicate themselves to celebrating Christ's prayer for His Body the Church in the Eucharist and the Liturgy of the Divine Office.

You will recall that before the great Battle of Lepanto [7 October 1571] between the Muslim Turks and the forces of Christendom, that St. Pius V called on all Christians to pray the Rosary for victory. It was this crusade of prayer that brought about the final victory and saved the church in Europe from being vanquished. Prayer has always worked in the past. It works now, and it will work in the future.

We in Magnificat are good at praying. St. Paul reminds us that the Holy Spirit is always interceding within us with "sighs too deep for words" [Romans 8:26]. Let us then ask the Holy Spirit to give us a finely tuned awareness of how we should pray for the Church and for the world.

As always, you are in my prayers and you are remembered at the Table of the Lord.

September 2017

Fr. Kevin Scallon, our CST Spiritual Advisor for the past 16 years, will be retiring from this role on October 4, 2017. We are very grateful to Fr. Kevin for his prayers and wisdom, for the Masses he said for Magnificat's intentions each week, for his inspiring Newsletter articles, wonderful Irish humor and too many other contributions to list! We can never thank him enough for his love and dedication to the ministry from the beginning, over 35 years ago!

We are delighted Fr. Kevin is one of the nineteen contributing authors in our second book in the Magnificat Proclaims series called Holy Orders, A Collection of Inspiring Clergy Testimonies. To read more about the life of this very special man, treat yourself to this amazing book which debuts at our Conference this October.

After much prayer and discernment, the CST offered this important role to Msgr. David Toups, Rector and President of the St. Vincent de Paul Seminary in Boynton Beach, FL. Msgr. Toups whole-heartedly accepted the invitation to become our new CST Spiritual Advisor and will assume this role on October 5, 2017, feast day of St. Faustina and the opening of the Magnificat Conference.

We praise God for both of these holy & generous priests and ask that you keep them in your prayers.

OTHER PUBLICATIONS BY
MAGNIFICAT CENTRAL SERVICE TEAM

Magnificat Proclaims (Available in English and Spanish)
Our first book in the Magnificat Proclaims series is a collection of nineteen powerful and inspiring testimonies given at Magnificat Meals around the world. The contributing authors are Annette Baber, Diane Bates, Kathleen Beckman, Johnnette Benkovic, Babsie Bleasdell, Dorinda Bordlee, Kitty Cleveland, Sharon Lee Giganti, Marilyn Heap, Elizabeth Kim, Kathy MacInnis, Sr. Briege Mckenna, O.S.C., Patti Mansfield, Rosalind Moss, Marilyn Quirk, Elyse O'Kane, Carol Razza, Jan Tate, and Maria Vadia.

Magnificat Proclaims—Holy Orders
This second book in the Magnificat Proclaims series features nineteen of our clergy who have shared their personal journey at a Magnificat Meal. The contributing authors are Bishop Barber, Fr. Barry, Fr. Calloway, Fr. Cantalamessa, Fr. Cerulli, Fr. Cohen, Archbishop Cordileone, Fr. Crowley, Msgr. Doktorczyk, Fr. Hampsch, Bishop Jacobs, Deacon Jones, Fr. Montague, Fr. Nguyen, Fr. Skonezny, Fr. Scallon, Fr. Struzzo, Fr. Thai, and Msgr. Toups.

Woman, Called By Name—For Such A Time As This
This Bible study consists of a facilitator and participant workbook and has received the Nihil Obstat and Imprimatur. The facilitator workbook includes twenty lessons (ten Old Testament and ten New Testament) with questions and answers, seven CDs with the twenty audio teachings, and one Music CD with songs and printed lyrics to complement each lesson. The participant workbook includes the same twenty lessons (ten Old Testament and ten New Testament) with questions for reflection and printed song lyrics to complement each lesson. The ten Old Testament lessons feature: the Creation of Woman, Sarah, Rebekah, Rachel and Leah, Deborah and Jael, Hannah, Judith and The Worthy Wife. The ten women featured in the New Testament are Elizabeth, The Samaritan Woman, The Woman Caught in Adultery, Mary Magdalene, Martha and Mary, Mary of Bethany, Herodias and Her Daughter, Women Touched by Jesus, Salome, Mother of James and John, and Mary, Mother of Jesus.

Woman, Called By Name
This journal opens wide the door to personal prayer through Scripture-based meditations of women in the Bible from both the Old and New Testaments.

Journey with Mary
This journal opens wide the door to personal prayer through Scripture-based meditations that help us to contemplate the life of our Blessed Mother, who is the role model for all Christians.

A Guide to Presenting Life in the Spirit for Youth
One of the greatest things a parent (or grandparent) can give a child is the gift of the knowledge of God's love and the power and anointing of the Holy Spirit. This booklet is a simple guide on how to conduct a Life in the Spirit (LIS) for Youth. It is designed to take place in a home setting, in small groups with the parents as teachers. The lessons are designed for youth (with some minor adjustments for age differences) from ages four through sixteen. They are offered in one to four sessions depending on the time available and the attention and maturity level of the participants.

For ordering information, visit our website at
www.magnificat-ministry.org.

Magnificat

PROCLAIMS

HOLY ORDERS
A Collection of Inspiring Clergy Testimonies

Fr. Kevin Scallon's personal testimony can be found in the Holy Orders book. If you're looking for an amazing read, don't miss this opportunity. Order today!

Fr. Kevin Scallon, C.M.

Received by Our Lord
June 25, 2018

"'Say a prayer for me, Father' is a request commonly made by people to a priest; and if I say to someone 'I will pray for you,' even though they may not be strong believers, they are always delighted ... As always, you are in my prayers and you are remembered at the Table of the Lord."